'The author shines a laser-like, bright li fragmented landscape called the English sch< some pathways that, if taken, could lead t< and future generations, and helpfully signp route. Accessible, principled, with realistic examples and always thought-provoking, this book is a must for school leaders, policymakers and academics alike.'

Professor Sir Tim Brighouse, Norham Fellow, University of Oxford, and formerly Commissioner for London Schools

'At a time of significant educational turmoil it is important that policymakers, teachers and researchers are provided with insightful interpretations of the changing landscape. In writing this book Richard Riddell has produced a well-balanced reflection of the potential impact of these current changes, and raises pertinent questions about the veracity of the political motivations and theories driving this agenda. At the heart of this important book is an empathy for teachers, presented with a realistic perspective of the challenges faced by schools in the twenty-first century. This book will surely be essential reading for all who wish to engage in an informed debate about educational policy and its impact upon the teaching profession.'

Richard Rose, Professor of Inclusive Education, University of Northampton

Equity, Trust and the Self-improving Schools System

To dearest Millie

To Nick
with best wishes
Richard
March 2016

Equity, Trust and the Self-improving Schools System

Richard Riddell

is an imprint of

First published in 2016 by the UCL Institute of Education Press, University College London, 20 Bedford Way, London WC1H 0AL

ioepress.co.uk

British Library Cataloguing in Publication Data:
A catalogue record for this publication is available from the British Library

ISBNs
978-1-85856-692-4 (paperback)
978-1-85856-693-1 (PDF eBook)
978-1-85856-694-8 (ePub eBook)
978-1-85856-695-5 (Kindle eBook)

Typeset by Quadrant Infotech (India) Pvt Ltd
Printed by CPI Group (UK) Ltd, Croydon, CR0 4YY

Cover image © Andronikos Zantis/EyeEm.

Contents

List of figures

List of terms and abbreviations

The most recent period of reforms has engendered a range of new abbreviations and other terms. I have explained most of these when first used in the book but the following list may also help.

ADCS	Association of Directors of Children's Services
ASCL	Association of School and College Leaders – a trades union representing senior staff in schools and colleges
Building Schools for the Future	A major capital development scheme introduced under the Labour Government but scrapped by the incoming Coalition in 2010
CAF	Common Assessment Framework
CPD	Continuing Professional Development
DfE	Department for Education, the central government department in London responsible for school policy in England. Its predecessors were the Department for Children, Schools and Families (2007–10), the Department for Education and Skills (2001–07), the Department for Education and Employment (1995–2001) and, before 1995, the DfE again.
EFA	Education Funding Agency
Ever6FSM	The measure for disadvantage that includes all students who have claimed free school meals at any time during the previous six years
EPPSE	Effective Pre-school, Primary and Secondary Education project, formerly EPPE before it included secondary
HMI	The crown-appointed professional staff of Ofsted, all of whom have teaching experience
HTB	Headteacher Advisory Board (to Regional Schools Commissioners)
IDACI	Income Deprivation Affecting Children Index
Inspection Service Provider	A private-sector organization contracted with Ofsted to provide school inspections until 31 August 2015
Key Stages	Since the introduction of the National Curriculum by legislation in 1988, the schooling of children in

England is divided into Key Stage 1 (ages 5–7), Key Stage 2 (7–11), Key Stage 3 (11–14) and Key Stage 4 (14–16). Key Stage 5 is sometimes used to refer to post-16 education and Key Stage 1 is preceded by the Early Years Foundation Stage.

LA	local authority
LGA	Local Government Association
LLE	Local Leader of Education
MAT	Multi-academy Trust
NAO	National Audit Office
NCTL	National College for Teaching and Leadership (formerly National College for School Leadership or NCSL)
NLE	National Leader of Education
NPQH	National Professional Qualification for Headship
NSN	The New Schools Network – an independent organization historically funded by the DfE to support free school applications
NSS	National Support School
OECD	Organisation for Economic Co-operation and Development
Ofsted	Originally the Office for Standards in Education, now the Office for Standards in Education, Children's Services and Skills; technically a non-ministerial department of the UK Government; carries out inspections of schools in England
PFI	Public Finance Initiative – a mechanism for providing capital funding for public service building projects whereby, in general, the private sector builds and maintains a new school or groups of schools in return for a regular payment over 25 years or more
RI	Requires Improvement – the Ofsted judgement that replaced 'Satisfactory' in 2012
RSC	Regional Schools Commissioner
SENCO	Special Educational Needs Coordinator (for a school)
SEND	Special Educational Needs and Disability
SIA	School Improvement Adviser
SIP	School Improvement Partner
SLE	Specialist Leader of Education
SOLACE	Society of Local Authority Chief Executives
SPAG	Spelling, Punctuation and Grammar

Teach First   A charity set up to provide intensive two-year programmes of initial teacher education in partnership with universities. Unlike most universities, it has a commitment to 'end educational inequality'. Trainees commence teaching after six weeks of intensive training.

TSA   Teaching School Alliance

Pseudonyms of frequently quoted interviewees

It seemed sensible to give pseudonyms to some interviewees to avoid having to introduce them each time I quote or refer to them. I have not allocated pseudonyms to the many interviewees I draw on infrequently or do not quote at all.

I provide just enough detail here, I hope, to protect anonymity while informing the reader:

Alan is a well-known campaigner on academy matters.

Alison is a longstanding well-positioned head of a large primary school (three forms of entry) in a town in a unitary authority. Her school was rated 'outstanding' several years ago and is maintained. She is an NLE.

Andrew is the head of a primary academy serving a deprived area. His school is outstanding and he is well positioned.

Arthur is the headteacher of a smaller primary school in a shire county. His school was rated 'Good' by Ofsted and is maintained.

Adrian is the Director of Children's Services in a small unitary authority serving communities of various backgrounds and means. He has additional responsibilities.

Cameron is an ex-primary head of a large urban primary school, ex-HMI and working as a contracted school improvement adviser.

Catherine is the Director of Children's Services in a shire county serving market towns and rural areas. She has extra responsibilities.

Charles is a senior second-tier education officer in an urban metropolitan authority.

Charlotte was an Additional Inspector who worked with schools as a consultant in various parts of the country, mainly for a national academy chain at the time of the interview.

Daniel is the head of a regionally focused academy chain with six secondary schools at the time of my visit. The chain has since extended its remit.

Dominic is the head of a four-school academy chain in the south west. He is a former secondary head and deputy headteacher, a member of the regional headteacher board and an LLE.

Douglas is a senior adviser in an urban LA and was an Additional Inspector. He has extensive secondary management experience and has served in a number of interim roles.

Edwin is the principal of a free school in West London.

Jack is the headteacher of a primary school serving a large area of housing. His school requires improvement and is an academy.

James is the head of the largest academy chain I visited.

Jean works as a manager for an Inspection Service Provider.

Joan was an Additional Inspector and ex-senior primary adviser in an urban unitary authority in the south east. She does extensive consultancy in London, including as a contracted school improvement adviser.

Julian is a consultant with extensive experience in LAs and the private sector.

Leonard is the coordinator of a learning community and a previous longstanding headteacher of an outstanding primary school.

Marion is the headteacher of a primary school in London and Teaching School that will soon have five forms of entry. She had just stepped down as Executive Head of another neighbouring primary school. Her school is outstanding and she is an inspector.

Mark is a Teach First graduate and former secondary teacher who works with free schools.

Martin is the headteacher of a secondary school serving a deprived area. His school has recently been judged good and is maintained.

Michael is the headteacher of a one-form-entry primary school in a town in the south west. His school is outstanding and he is a lead inspector and an LLE.

Peter is the head of a secondary academy, an early converter that had been outstanding for ten years when I interviewed him. He is an NLE and well positioned.

Richard is the head of a secondary faith school. It is outstanding and maintained. He is an NLE.

Thomas is the head of a secondary school in a shire county serving a small town and a rural catchment. His school is outstanding and he is an NLE.

Apologies to my interviewees for these pseudonyms and to all those I have not quoted. That would take another book.

Acknowledgements

I have many people to thank who have helped in the writing of this book. In it, I return to some of my basic personal and professional passions after 40 years of working in state education: how schools can get better, and how they can improve the outcomes for all children, particularly the disadvantaged. And how, in turn, schools might contribute to making our society a better place than it is now – something that has motivated me, and so many others I know, since I stepped off my teaching practice bus for the first time and caught sight of my first comprehensive school.

My thinking has developed in unanticipated ways since starting the work for this book in 2013. Looking back at my notes and a paper I presented at the British Educational Research Association annual conference in 2014, the polity has also developed almost beyond recognition and some of the debates presented in these pages continue to move on rapidly.

The Bath Spa Institute for Education has been especially supportive and tolerant throughout my writing of this book. Not only was I allocated small research grants twice from its central QR research allocation, but I was also helped out by the Dean, Kate Reynolds, and my head of department, Alan Howe, when I took advantage of opportunities at extremely short notice to interview key players in the education polity and organize the transcripts.

And I must thank Suzanne Lawrence for producing the near-immaculate transcripts on which this book is based, sometimes from scratchy and buzzy telephone recordings. Anyone who has trawled through poor transcripts will know what I mean: reaching long passages that make so little sense that you cannot recall the conversation at all. I have *never* experienced this with Suzanne. She has saved me hours and hours and hours of work. Thank you, Suzanne.

I cannot name some of the people to whom I have spoken more than once because they must remain anonymous. But I can thank my old friend John Simpson who really does make me think every time I meet him, often leading me to change my mind. He will see some of his influence in these pages.

Several people have made helpful comments on aspects of the draft manuscript, including attributions, and sometimes recommending I look at other publications. Here, I must thank another old friend (yet again) David

James at Cardiff, but also Carol Vincent at the UCL Institute of Education and Steve Strand at Oxford. Geoff Whitty, Tim Brighouse and Sally Boulter made positive comments on various drafts and I must of course thank Geoff for his Foreword. David McGahey provided helpful background papers from his position within the polity. The work of many academic colleagues over the years has helped me come to an understanding of the shifting nature of policy formations in England (that perhaps have not changed much, you may think actually) and they are all acknowledged in the text.

I must also thank all the interviewees. If there is one clear story to emerge from the huge mountain of data collected from these interviews it is that headteachers remain passionate, committed and thoughtful about what might be best for their students, in all sorts of schools and in all sorts of communities. Spending time with them was always the great privilege of being a local authority officer. Thank you also to the chief and other senior officers who not only agreed to be interviewed but also suggested others whose views I might find interesting (not always positively!), and for letting me have access to a range of their documentation. The rewards and challenges of these jobs – and officers' commitment – remain as apparent as ever, but the ambiguities and complexities through which they have to steer are far more complex, in my view, compared with even the first and second terms of the Blair governments.

The polity now has more and more people in different roles compared to ten years ago, whether heads of chains or, more recently, Regional Schools Commissioners. All are passionate about the same things, persuasive and believe rightly that good schooling is fundamental to redressing the all-too-great disadvantages explored in detail in Chapter 1.

Thank you to my students at Bath Spa. I have shared some early drafts of texts for this book with Year 3 undergraduate and Master's Education Policy students to help them with their own work and research. As many of you will know, when you are teaching, you *cannot* leave ambiguities, you must be absolutely clear about the limits of what you are able to say and what you cannot. Many conversations in seminars and tutorials have helped me be clearer myself about what is important generally: a mature student's children had attended just a 'very ordinary' primary school, for example (therefore posing the question to us all of what we should do about it); and future teachers said they *did* want national expectations of schools raised and they *did* want to be 'ambitious for children', as the inspirational free school principal says in Chapter 4.

Acknowledgements

Finally, and as always, my grateful thanks to Gillian Klein for her patient and encouraging editing, seeing things I hadn't seen myself, and making this a much better book than it would have been otherwise.

Thank you all. The rest is down to me.

Richard Riddell
Burton, Wiltshire
September 2015

Foreword

I am delighted to have been asked to write the foreword to this book. Like Richard Riddell's earlier volumes on *Schools for Our Cities* (2003) and *Aspiration, Identity and Self-Belief* (2010), this accessible and thought-provoking book reflects a rare familiarity with both academic studies of education and the realities of educational policy and practice on the ground.

These characteristics are perhaps not surprising in view of Richard's unusual combination of experience as a local authority officer and as a researcher and teacher in universities. Having had the privilege of observing him at work in both contexts, I am full of admiration for his capacity to bring those two worlds together – as he has done so successfully in this book.

The book could well prove to be the definitive study of the education polity in the current era. Its refreshing take on the landscape of what David Bell has called a 'system of many small systems' is neither one of ecstatic enthusiasm nor one of total critique. He identifies both positive and negative aspects of this new educational order, in which he regards the new Regional Schools Commissioners as having a pivotal role.

While he probably shares the values of the critics rather than the advocates of recent reforms, his interest lies in where we might go from here. So, perhaps surprisingly for a former Director of Education, he does not hark back to a golden age of local authority hegemony in education. Rather he accepts the reality of the current changes, while not regarding them as the end point of reform.

In some ways, then, he sees the present situation as a way station on the road to a more desirable future where the benefits of new ways of working could just lead to a restoration of trust and confidence in teachers – and it is one in which he even posits a possible new role for local authorities in a school-led system.

While recognizing the not inconsiderable obstacles to such an outcome in current political circumstances, Richard Riddell's book can be read as an enticing plea to progressive stakeholders in education to work together towards the sort of imagined future that he himself is envisaging and advocating. Only time – and effort – will tell if that can be transformed into a real possibility.

Professor Geoff Whitty, CBE
Director Emeritus
UCL Institute of Education

About the author

Richard Riddell has worked for over forty years in, with and on state schooling. He has been a teacher in comprehensive schools, an officer in four local authorities (including seven years as Director of Education in a major UK city), a consultant in the private sector and joint head of education in an international NGO. He has taught at Bath Spa University since 2009. His lifelong passion has been the contribution schools can make to a better society, and to the reduction of England's chronic and endemic inequality. His previous books have examined the nature of schooling required in urban areas and the social basis and realization of aspiration.

Chapter 1

Equity and its dilemmas

Oxford University is world-famous for academic excellence. We pick the best and brightest students purely on their academic merit and passion for their chosen course. If that sounds like you, and you like to think for yourself, Oxford could be the right university for you.

(Oxford University Admissions website homepage)

... I agree there is a problem and I share your anger at it. Oxford should be a meritocracy where only the brightest and best attend regardless of their background.

(Student blog, *The Oxford Student*, May 2014)

Men make their own history, but they do not make it just as they please; they do not make it under circumstances chosen by themselves, but under circumstances directly encountered, given and transmitted from the past. The tradition of all the dead generations weighs like a nightmare on the brain of the living. And just when they seem engaged in revolutionising themselves and things, in creating something that has never yet existed, precisely in such periods of revolutionary crisis they anxiously conjure up the spirits of the past to their service and borrow from them names, battle-cries and costumes in order to present the new scene of world history in this time-honoured disguise and this borrowed language.

(Marx, 1979: 103–4)

Foundational questions

This book was largely written during the last year of the Coalition Government formed after the UK General Election in 2010 and finished during the first three months of the Conservative Government arising from the 2015 election.

The first coalition in the UK since the national unity government during the Second World War might have been expected to develop something of a compromise programme because of an inconclusive election result. But the programme it published in 2010 (Cabinet Office, 2010) led to five years of major structural reform for English schools that, as I argue in these pages, has been completely reconfiguring the education polity. By this I mean the distribution of power between schools and all the institutions that work with them in educating English children, together with the arrangements through which schools seek support, assistance and continuing motivation in their task. This continues with the new Government: with new legislation in 2015, I argue, an old system of oversight of school standards by local councils is largely, with a few exceptions, in the throes of passing away. There has been an 'effective collapse of local authority [school] improvement services' (Husbands, 2015: 32) that affects local authorities' other and wider roles.

I am going to document this reconfiguring and transforming polity, based on detailed critical readings of policy documentation, analyses by other academics of the developing 'landscape' for schooling (as Simkins *et al.*, 2014, term it) and above all my own continuing interviews with people working at various levels of the new polity. These include headteachers of academies, what we have now learned to call 'maintained' schools and a free school – the people who are living and interpreting the changes. I explain how these interviews have been organized, chosen, conducted and reported in Chapter 2. The foundational questions for this research were: how will the new system work for schools and how will it frame the work of teachers? And for both, how is this different from previous eras?

There is a deeper point, however, about the English education 'system'. I continue to use this word, contrary to Lawn's view that this is merely a 'vernacular device' (Lawn, 2013: 236), because the totality of schools in any country is subject to, and embedded in, demographic, political, cultural, social and economic forces that make their tasks generically similar and make them behave in similar and investigable ways. This is irrespective of how amenable they may or may not be to central bureaucratic influence from the state or other organizations such as teacher trade unions. In any case, all of them have to respond to the 'steering at a distance' provided through Ofsted (Ozga, 2009) that now, according to the interview data presented in the book, is much more closely aligned with the regional structure of the Department for Education (DfE). But I will show how Ofsted's role goes beyond steering now or even agenda-setting.

The English system has been producing some of the most inequitable outcomes for young people in the developed world (OECD, 2010), by social (class) and ethnic background and gender. I will set out some of the parameters of this inequity in some detail shortly; arguably, they may have narrowed slightly during the period of the UK Labour Government, particularly in the late 2000s (Whitty and Anders, 2013), and now seem to have been doing so again (NAO, 2015), but by no means evenly or straightforwardly (DfE, 2014a). One implication of this is that, in an age of credentialism, where legitimizing certification for the market is sought by individuals and organizations at all stages of their lives and trajectories, the composition of what we can now reasonably and objectively call the 'elite' (documented by Jones, 2014 and Savage *et al.*, 2013) – all those who decide the priorities and direction of our country – looks much as it did a generation ago. It has been tempered only by the accretion of different styles of dress and cultural tastes (Skeggs, 2004) so that its members are not always detectable or recognizable in public. I have argued elsewhere (Riddell, 2010) that this means our society, particularly in its social relations of power, influence and wealth, is unlikely to change even if wider economic and social benefits trickle down to everyone – which now seems unlikely seven years after the 'great recession' (Belfield *et al.*, 2014). This had been the trick of previous periods from 1945 to the mid-1970s (Dorling, 2014; Hobsbawm, 1995).

So, embedded as schools are in wider social and economic structures, there has been a further foundational question for this investigation: whether the continuing dramatic reforms we have experienced since 2010 are likely to enable schools to achieve greater equity for their children's outcomes and more effectively so than the organizational arrangements that preceded them. My answer at this stage of the polity is affirmative, though at varying rates of progress. There remain a number of dilemmas to resolve, however, including the very shape of the active state itself in a marketized yet managerialized conception of the world. Nevertheless, I argue that the development of a potentially consistent regional structure, in effect replacing the inconsistent local authority (LA) one, contains the seeds of possibility for achieving greater equity in England and, depending on how the dilemmas are resolved over the next few years, for an emerging infrastructure between schools that is based on trust and cooperation between teachers. LAs, if they wish, can have important roles in helping build this infrastructure.

Whatever the shape of the polity, changing what happens between seven and a half million children and over 400,000 teachers is never straightforward, as many Secretaries of State have discovered, and as Stephen Ball has consistently argued (from 1990 onwards). The point is that what is in place this year, 2015, frames what will happen for the next ten years and, in some cases, the next twenty to fifty, because of the irreversible nature of the changes that are taking place and because the endgame of attainment is about so much more than just passing exams. This is the argument for increasing social mobility made by the last government (Cabinet Office, 2011) and, by me, for elite transformation.

Some parameters of inequity in England
School, family and community
Schools are part of wider local, national and international systems and ecologies (Ozga, 2012); and education professionals are formed by the

institutions through which they train and develop, and in which they are managed and led. This is not to say that such processes are without resistance or reflection, or that schools are all the same (although many in England are very similar). It is just that schools and their staff are part of the wider contradictory developments and *histories* of the societies in which they serve and of which they are a part, and which they interpret in particular, local ways.

Similarly, as young people make the daily 'lateral transition' between home and school, as Hughes *et al.* (2010) term it, they bring into the school environment interpretative predispositions or *habitus* (Bourdieu and Wacquant, 1992), formed by the conflicts, tensions and happinesses of growing up in family and community. What happens at school enables their further development, conscious and subconscious, and they bring it back into the home.

Whereas school, and its end-credentials, are clearly important to young people, they spend variable amounts of time there, depending on where they live (see, for instance, OECD, 2012) and their own commitment and circumstances. There have been many attempts at calculating how much of their life young people spend in school – and hence, presumably (intentionally), the likely influence that school has on them. Taking the OECD figures and older calculations such as those of the US National Research Council (2000), it seems to be only about 14 or 15 per cent of their time. Even when set against the third of their time they spend asleep (*ibid.*), this represents a relatively small fraction of the influences surrounding young people as they grow up, if we consider just the time element and leave aside the question of how young people manage their various identities, as Hughes *et al.* term it; or indeed the conflicts between their identities and the congruence between the home learning environments (Sylva *et al.*, 2010) their parents or family provide and those they experience in school.

Economic inequity

So schools and students are firmly planted in a wider society that is an unequal and unjust place. Children and schools will experience this wider world differently – and in some cases, wildly differently. First, in pure economic terms, the current generation of parents has been shaped by a prolonged, though not even, process of growing inequality. Unemployment began to emerge again as a major social issue in the early 1970s (Brown and Lauder, 1997), for the first time since the 1930s, and the period from the mid-to-late 1970s to the 1990s saw growing regional and social disparities. By 1994, British society could be described as one in 'decline, with a weak economy, high unemployment and rising inequality' (Lawton *et al.*, 2014: 20). There were gains in terms of reducing poverty during the period of the UK Labour Government (1997–2010), with middle income groups moving towards higher income groups, at least until the mid-2000s (Hills *et al.*, 2009). Yet for the lowest income groups there were no such gains in relative terms: while the gap between the richest and the poorest during that time did not increase, nor did it get any narrower.

A 2002 study by the Institute for Fiscal Studies (cited in Belfield *et al.*, 2014: 1) reported 'robust year-on-year growth in living standards' at that time, and 'falling levels of poverty', albeit accompanied by rising inequality. Six years after the 'great recession' in 2008, however, Bellfield *et al.* went on to document that income had begun to stabilize after six years of decline. A telling statistic is that relative poverty appeared to be at a lower level in 2013 (their latest figures) because of the fall in average wage levels. Nevertheless, because of differentially changing housing costs, the poorest had become worse off because their housing costs had not fallen as much as those for higher income groups. This does not take into consideration the changes being introduced into the benefits system (DWP, 2015), in the form of capping housing benefits during 2012–13 for some families and tougher sanctions for claimants of out-of-work benefits, including Job Seekers' Allowance (JSA). This move could subtract over £100 a week for some families (Bellfield *et al.*, 2014). In addition, annual benefits increases are now fixed at less than inflation. There are more changes promised at the time of writing (DWP, 2015), including cash-capping of the overall benefits being received by individual households.

When the UK Coalition Government came to power in 2010, income inequality was in any case at its highest for thirty years (Brewer *et al.*, 2009), before the income stabilization noted by Bellfield *et al.* (2014) and these mid-stream benefit changes. One measure of the increasing income (as opposed to wealth) inequality is shown by Danny Dorling's (2014) calculation that, if the National Minimum Wage (required by law for over 21 year-olds in the UK) had kept pace with the rise in salaries of the chief executives of the top FTSE 100 companies since 1999, it would have been £18.89 per hour as opposed to the £6.19 it actually was. Inequality in itself is seen to be significant, but Bellfield *et al.* (2014) say that *absolute* poverty, which is a real-terms comparison as opposed to the relative measure which shifts with changing overall median income levels, is now at its highest for ten years, with rises concentrated in working households. Generally, the real-terms income pressure has been felt less by pensioners recently than by working families with children.

Poverty and its effects

In terms of the numbers, this means that there were 3.2 million children (24.1 per cent) living with material deprivation during 2012–13 (the latest figures available at the time of writing), with an increase of 300,000 during that year alone. Material deprivation is measured in terms of what families say they cannot afford, ranging from 'severe' (no warm winter coat) to 'less severe' (no annual one-week holiday). In addition, 15.9 per cent of households in 2014 had no one in work (ONS, 2014), but this figure has been falling, presumably related to the apparent uptake of lower-paid or part-time employment (ONS, 2015). Nevertheless, these overall figures mask considerable variations by region and ethnic group (SMCP, 2014).

As far as poverty is concerned, what might begin as an indicator of material deprivation or absolute poverty begins to have social effects. Tess Ridge (2006) documents how children voluntarily withdraw from certain activities, such as school trips, even when schools are able to pay their expenses, rather than owning up to needing help or asking their parents. Out of school, those teenagers who do not have the range of clothes they feel they need to socialize with their peers will often avoid such socializing. More recently, Holloway *et al.* (2014), 'Children's Commissioners', document how 'two thirds of children in families who are "not well off" said they were embarrassed because they couldn't afford *a* cost of school' (*ibid*: 9 – my emphasis). More than a quarter, according to this survey, had been bullied as a consequence. Specifically, they mention school uniform – this may be heightened because of the 'rediscovered traditions' of blazers, expensive badges and ties (Whitty, 2002) – plus school meals, materials, trips (again) and, expected by the school for homework, access to the internet. All these are considered necessary for full participation in school and social life.

More broadly, the National Children's Bureau, pursuing its historic mission, published its call for *Greater Expectations* (NCB, 2013) because children experiencing poverty and disadvantage, or living in disadvantaged areas, are more likely to be born underweight, be obese, suffer accidental injuries at home, live in poor or overcrowded conditions and have less access to green space and places to play. If the UK were doing as well as the 'best industrialized countries', they say that 770,000 fewer children would be living in poor environmental conditions, one million fewer would be living in poverty and 172 fewer would die each year (*ibid*: 1). Moreover, these disadvantages are *cumulative* – the lower the child's socio-economic status at birth (not quite the same as low income), the greater the likelihood of their experiencing multiple deprivation by the age of 30 (Feinstein *et al.*, 2007), measured as eight out of ten indicators.

Income inequality and its effects

These are the different experiences – and risks – for children living in poverty, before we consider what they bring to school with them each morning and what they get out of it after 13 years of compulsory education. The experiences of children and young people differ more broadly, however, when we look beyond those suffering measured material deprivation or living in poverty. Although absolute or relative poverty measures *absences* in children's lives, the very fact of income inequality, for example measured through the Gini coefficient, appears to have wider social and physical effects that implicate higher socio-economic groups than just the poor. Income inequality itself is seen as *at least associated* with these effects. In their ground-breaking 2009 book, *The Spirit Level*, Wilkinson and Pickett document significant differences in physical and mental health, community life, life expectancy, violence, imprisonment and social mobility associated with inequality – not just poverty – before considering the differences in educational attainment that are the focus of the present book. By looking at inequality, they are measuring a social gradient, they say, or hierarchy. Dorling (2014) also explores the wider inequalities of health and well-being that accompany income inequality.

It does not follow, of course, that pursuing redistributive tax policies or increasing benefits or transfers to reduce the inequality would quickly or even necessarily bring about changes in these wider social inequalities, even if they could be agreed and implemented. But arguments have been developed more broadly to show that inequality is the very *motor* of wider social forces internationally. Inequality in income may actually be flatlining in the UK now (Bellfield *et al.*, 2014) but the OECD documented that inequality across *all* OECD countries in 2011 (OECD, 2011a) had been rising for a considerable time. The measure it uses is a comparison between the top 10 per cent of earners and the bottom 10 per cent. The UK summary pages (OECD, 2011b) showed – as noted by Hills *et al.* (2009) – a decline in inequality in the early 2000s but a rise setting in from about 2005 onwards. The overall trend had been up since the mid-1970s, reflecting changes in OECD countries generally. Inequality in the UK in 2010 was also higher than the average for OECD countries (a Gini coefficient of over 0.34 compared to 0.31), but lower than that for the United States (0.37).

No doubt some readers of this book regard such inequalities as morally or politically wrong, and unjust because of who receives the benefits of this inequality and who does not. But Cingano, one of many to argue from econometric analysis, says that the long-term rising inequality in OECD countries has a 'negative and statistically significant effect on subsequent growth' (Cingano, 2014: 6). This has consequences for most of us. His argument is that the significant driver is the gap between low income households and the rest of the population, not higher income groups pulling away from the rest. The basis of this, according to him, is the depressed skills development ('human capital') in low income groups, which is a key factor in the low educational attainment of their children (Connolly *et al.*, 2014). Besides redistributive policies, active labour market policies and childcare and in-work benefits (mentioned earlier), Cingano advocates equality of opportunity in access to education. This book looks at what this might mean.

There are other economic arguments about the wider effects of income inequality. In a detailed analysis, Dorling (2010; 2014) argues that there is a sort of displacement factor at work: for example, the fact that the richest 1 per cent take 20 per cent of the country's income means that they cost 19 per cent above what it would cost to give them an 'equal share' (2014: 18). This, according to Dorling, is the price of the rich. Further, three times as much is being spent per child in the private schools sector, 'more than anywhere else in the world' (*ibid*: 40): £3.57 per child out of every £100 spent on secondary education, leaving just £0.80 per child for the remaining 93 per cent of children who attend state schools. These schools, Dorling argues, are unsurprisingly inferior, and their children are more likely to drop out early, less likely to be socially mobile and so forth. This reflects Cingano's argument: there are elements of human capital theory here too!

Entitlement, IQism and coming from good stock
Although Dorling says it is difficult to assess when the price of the rich becomes too 'burdensome' (2014: 18), as there will always be some price, he surely identifies correctly that those who benefit from inequality believe they *deserve* to have such a proportion of the national wealth and income. This is partly because they believe they really are the best, by both genetic and monetary inheritance. Their children attend the best schools and go to top, selective or 'prestigious' universities (Riddell, 2010) – hence the quotation from the Oxford University website at the beginning of this chapter. If, at this early stage of your life, you really believe you have achieved 'the brightest and the best' status, then of course you will also assume, however

subconsciously, that you deserve to be in charge and running things for the rest your life. This is habitus again. And your parents also assume and/ or tell you this. A sense of entitlement develops, and the existence of the wider social networks that enable you to enter elite professional careers, with parental monetary support if needed (Milburn, 2009; 2012), confirms these beliefs.

In this sense, Dorling is right about what the money spent on education might enable young people to achieve and be. In a memorable article from 2007, Vincent and Ball describe first how parents regard their children as having particular talents or attributes (for example, musicality) that may *entitle* or *require* them to have access to certain provision (private schools), while forgetting that five or more years of instrumental teaching *should* have such an effect, or else their money was not well spent. I have documented such expressed entitlements myself (2010), not only among parents who have already chosen the private education sector (largely at the age of 11 in the schools I was interviewing in), but also elsewhere. I have identified a common narrative on a variety of 'mums' websites' (to which 'dads' contribute) that (state) primary schools could not meet their (bright) children's needs, even at the age of 4.

There are some core beliefs underpinning such a sense of entitlement and self-worth. 'IQism', the belief that people have a fixed and measurable 'ability', predominates among the elite, according to Dorling, despite the lack of objective, independent evidence to this effect. He (2010: 46) points out that the construction of the distribution of ability shown in the OECD report (2007), for example, is actually predicated on the *prior* assumption of a normal distribution. Belief in the bell curve, or this normal distribution of talent, means that as the elite will be found towards the right-hand tip of the curve, they deserve to be running things.

And belief in IQism is not confined to the elite. Gillborn and Youdell, in another classic study (2000), found just such essentialist beliefs about children to be underpinning discriminatory practices in a state secondary school, denying black boys access to the higher GCSE papers, that is, those that carried the higher grades. Arguably, these beliefs in fixed ability are a peculiarly 'English disease', the ideological and philosophical root of such terms as the (as yet undiscovered) 'gifted' or 'talented' (Riddell, 2010). IQism represents, according to Ball, the 'nexus of psychology and eugenics' (Ball, 2013: 7).

The point is that, whereas the elite – the 1 per cent – may thus have a set of beliefs by which they justify their own position, many of these are shared in much wider strata of society, such as in the teaching profession.

This is the pernicious nature of IQism. Many consider that it is just the very brightest and best that make their way to the 'best' universities, with all its implications for future access to wealth, influence and power (see Power and Whitty, 2008, as well as Dorling, 2014) – ignoring the financial and cultural leg-up many of them have had on the way, as well as the extensive range of extra-curricular activities, including private tutors at key transition times. For example, a head of Sixth Form in a well-known independent school (Merryweather, which advertises itself as being for the 'top 5%' of boys), whom I interviewed previously (see Riddell, 2010), expressed the following view:

> You do say that Oxbridge graduates have ... more power, or whatever it is, but that's presumably why they got into Oxbridge, because they're the sort of people who have that facility, who have that ability. It's not the fact that they're Oxbridge graduates, it's the fact that they're very bright, hard-working people ... that's why they go to Oxbridge and end up in those positions ...
>
> (Head of Sixth Form, Merryweather Boys' School)

In other words, it is the best people who go there. According to Dorling, many people feel we are governed by the fittest, who should therefore be at the top. He expresses his incredulity that notions of being from the 'best stock' should still have currency in the twenty-first century.

HOW STUDENTS SEE IT ...

This is not necessarily quite how all students who succeeded in getting in to Oxbridge view the matter. An elected student union official, campaigning for a more diverse student body at his university, who had attended a private school himself, affirmed in an interview that he 'just knew so many people [at Oxbridge] who had no idea of the tiny percentage of the population they represented and how skewed the educational disparity in this country makes young people.' But he was clear how it had happened, and said many other students agreed with him: what he knew about 'schools like mine' was that they 'were absolute factories for getting people in here ... machines that were very finely tuned and very effective ...' and that 'we are operating in an environment that has set up this huge industry'. This is social structure at work.

... AND SOCIAL EXCLUSION

But Dorling (2010; 2014), who is also now at Oxbridge, documents how the elite's belief in their own deservedness leads, on the one hand, to regarding it as natural to *exclude* others – from educational, social and employment opportunities (he gives the example of not being able to live in the centre of English cities, particularly London). On the other, he says, it results in *justification* of the mechanisms by which their wealth and influence are maintained: successfully seeking tax relief (for example on profits and wealth) and economic policy advantages (for example, the relaxation of planning restrictions or access to lucrative public sector markets [see also Ball, 2007]). This is accompanied by making donations to particular political parties or being technically resident in offshore tax havens. As Owen Jones takes up the theme in *The Establishment* (2014), greed becomes good and is seen as the natural mechanism for wealth creation which, he argues, is good for everybody – a 'rising tide lifts all boats'. Jones documents, in addition, how the stories presented about the rich, through the 'mediaocracy', who are socially intimate with members of the establishment, not only show them in a good light but also defend them. A famous example was when the *Financial Times* said in 2009 that quite enough bankers had been prosecuted and it was time to stop (Jones, 2014: 269).

There are some differences in what is being measured that we must note at this point. The OECD (Cingano, 2014) measure is between the top and bottom deciles of income. Dorling's (2014) is between the top 1 per cent and the rest, and in other parts of his book the rest of the top decile who in effect help maintain the position of the top 1 per cent, with some degree of greater sacrifice on their part. And Savage *et al.* (2013), in an article written following the BBC's *Great British Class Survey*, identified that about 6 per cent of British Society could be classified from their responses as the 'elite', though the approach of this article has been heavily criticized by many, including Bradley (2014).

But Jones is interested in those overlapping (unnumbered) 'powerful groups that need to protect their position in a democracy' (Jones, 2014: 4) and that represent 'the institutional and intellectual means by which such a wealthy elite defends its interests' (*ibid*: 294). The Establishment – the elite – and their supporters are represented across industry and commerce, banking, politics and the media. There are strong echoes here, supporting Jones's hypothesis, of the question underlying Anthony Sampson's series of books on *The Anatomy of Britain* (the latest came out in 2004 just before his death), namely: 'Who runs this place?'

So entry to this elite, at least in England, is constrained by the mechanisms of wealth, inheritance and singular educational experience and access. Yet it remains sometimes invisible, as Jones argues, or at least well defended, with responsibility for society's ills being assigned to the unworthy poor and others. Thus the shape and colour of the elite seem unlikely to change unless some of these mechanisms behind this power – such as how educational attainment is conferred on young people – are altered.

Although the targets of these various observations may vary – size, income or power, for instance – there are sufficient common data and approaches to say that English society is unequal; that this is not changing and may be getting worse; that there is a wide range of social inequalities that complement those defined by income, and that all these are shored up by unequal access to power and institutions, increasingly by birth.

Equity in English schools
The focus on outcomes
It is within this wider context of social and economic inequality that the success or otherwise of English state schools, attended by 93 per cent of children, must be set and considered. One prominently expressed political view is that schools are, or should be, the 'engines of social mobility' as the former Secretary of State for Education in England, Michael Gove, said (DfE, 2010a: 6). So a background issue for this book – to which I return – is therefore whether schools by themselves, working within the wider context of inequality, are able to make a significant contribution to widening opportunities, or need to rely on broader social and economic policies that help change the context around them. Children, as noted earlier, bring this wider experience of inequality, articulated or not, into school every day through their 'lateral transition'.

Nevertheless, the prime focus for this investigation is on measured attainment outcomes. These are important *individual social markers* at transitional points: from home to an early years setting, from there to schooling, from school to college or university, or at any time to further training and employment. Across what the Coalition Government called the 'life cycle' (Cabinet Office, 2011), attainment outcomes are also *measures* of individual functioning that might be important to make transitions successfully. This is controversial because of its alleged dire effects on schooling (Coffield and Williamson, 2011).

But measure for measure, the overall picture for inequality in English schools *is* poor – there are 'long-standing patterns of unequal outcomes … with children from poorer backgrounds [being] less successful than their more advantaged peers in tests in a range of subjects' (Kerr and West, 2010: 10). Schools do reflect society. Further, these social differences are much more pronounced in England than in many developed countries (OECD, 2010); what Lawton *et al.* describe as educational 'failure' (2014: 32) has not been tackled. The association between socio-economic background and attainment, together with other related outcomes such as university attendance, is well attested and much written-about (see DCSF, 2009b; Hills *et al.*, 2010; Gregg and Goodman, 2010; Clifton and Cook, 2012; NCB, 2013). And as the National Audit Office says, in life cycle terms, 'poor academic performance is associated with lower wages and higher unemployment in adulthood ... The attainment gap is [thus] a *key mechanism for transmitting poverty* from one generation to another' (NAO, 2015: 5 – my emphasis).

The outcome data gaps

It all begins before school. One of the most memorable graphs cited in the 2009 compilation on deprivation undertaken under the Labour Government (DCSF, 2009b: 34), from Feinstein, is reproduced in Figure 1.1. It is intended to show that children with high levels of cognitive functioning at the age of 22 months but from low socio-economic status (SES) backgrounds, are overtaken by children from higher SES backgrounds with lower levels of cognitive functioning at 22 months, during Key Stage 1 (when they are about 6 years old). And, by the time they approach the end of primary schooling, a rank order of cognitive functioning is also much more a socio-economic one. This powerful graph is also commented on by Whitty and Anders (2013: 6) and in the Cabinet Office publication (2011):

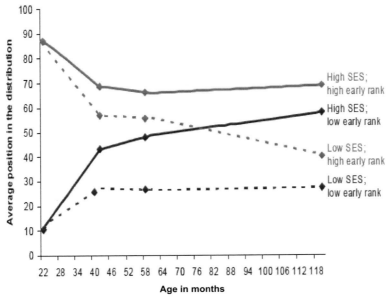

Figure 1.1: Differential trajectory of children by socio-economic group from 22 to 118 months

(DCSF, 2009b: 34)

13

It should be said that interpretation of this particular graph needs to be extremely cautious as it may overstate the gap. Jerrim and Vignoles (2011) argue that what is shown graphically here results from a statistical artefact whereby repeated measurement of a variable leads to values that regress to the mean over time.

Nevertheless, that there is an apparent long-term trajectory in outcomes is also observed by the Social Mobility and Child Poverty (SMCP) Commission, set up by the Coalition Government to oversee its eponymous strategies, and others. In its *State of the Nation* report (2014) it states that not only are 'poor children four times as likely to become poor adults as other children' (*ibid*: iv), but also 'two thirds of children who are eligible for free school meals … are not ready for school at the age of five'. In other words, these children are deemed not to have achieved a 'good level of development' in the Early Years Foundation Stage (*ibid*: 31), as opposed to 48 per cent of other children. Further, they are less likely to experience an 'excellent education' than their peers at the next stage of their trajectories, or be 'taught by the best teachers' (*ibid*: xxi). The DfE (2014d) points out in one of its statistical releases that 67 per cent of 'disadvantaged pupils' (by which it means children eligible for free school meals during the past six years, the Ever6FSM measure) achieved the combined expected level in reading, writing and mathematics by the end of their primary schooling, as opposed to 83 per cent of all other children – a gap of 16 percentage points, though this had narrowed over the previous two years by 2 per cent.

And for 16-year-olds, during the previous year (the measure available at the time), there had been no reduction in the gap between the 62 per cent of poor children, as the SMCP points out in its report, who failed to achieve the benchmark measure for 16-year-olds of five GCSEs at grades A*–C including English and Maths (or 5ACEM as this is known), and the 35 per cent of young people overall. A year later, according to the (revised) first statistical release from the DfE in 2014 (DfE, 2014e), some 33.5 per cent of disadvantaged pupils achieved the 5ACEM measure, as opposed to 64 per cent of all other pupils, leaving a gap of 30.5 points, albeit on a revised methodology.

There are also lower percentages of disadvantaged children making the expected progress, as it has come to be known, in English and Mathematics. And when alternatively applying the Income Deprivation Affecting Children Index (IDACI), which relates to place of residence rather than school attended (not always the same, especially in urban areas), the 5ACEM gap ranges, by region, from 41.6 per cent in the East of England, to 26.3 per cent in London. The most recently published figures on this gap show that, despite a 4.7 percentage-point reduction in the gap for primary schools between 2011 and 2014, and one of 1.6 percentage points at secondary, the 'gap remains wide' (NAO, 2015: 10).

There are considerations about comparability between measures here, as the National Audit Office says, ranging from the revised reported performance measures for 11-year-olds to the exclusion of a range of vocational qualifications from the secondary tables in 2014. And these figures do not relate to, or measure, the same children. But they do affirm that this gap – the target of policy for all recent Governments – has apparently widened between the end of primary education and the crucial staging post of age 16, five years later, when students will decide (and may or may not be qualified for) the next step in their educational, occupational and, of course, social and economic trajectories.

The various measures used by the DfE statistical releases relate to forms of *deprivation*, which is sometimes the same as measures of income inequality, but the social trajectory of attainment, including that of young people who could not be considered deprived at all, is also well established. Another graphic illustration is given in the DCSF document (2009b: 46), reproduced in Figure 1.2.

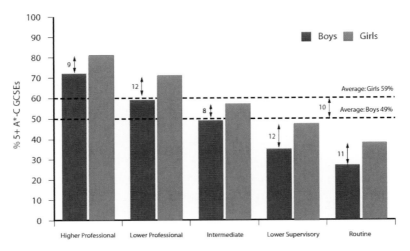

Figure 1.2: Percentage of pupils gaining 5+ A*–Cs by gender and occupational class (2004)

(DCSF, 2009b: 45)

On this older measure of 5A*–C grades at GCSE, the social gradient in attainment between the children of higher professionals and working-class backgrounds is steep, and this will have been reflected in later trajectories because of the nature of these key qualifiers. The gender gap is also interesting here, though only the girls from 'routine' backgrounds (less- or un-skilled working class) outperform boys from a higher socio-economic group.

Finally, the attainment gaps by ethnic group reinforce the prime focus of this book on social background and the advantages and disadvantages it confers. The last graph from the DCSF document (2009b: 21) is shown in Figure 1.3.

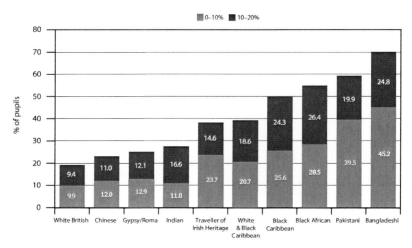

Figure 1.3: Percentage of pupils living in the 20% most deprived postcode areas as defined by the Index of Multiple Deprivation (2005) (DCSF, 2009b: 20)

Figure 1.3 shows the percentage of pupils, by ethnic group, living in the 20 per cent most deprived postcode areas as defined by the Index of Multiple Deprivation (2005), yet another measure used by UK Government statisticians, incorporating a wider range of indicators than the IDACI. This demonstrates that 70 per cent of Bangladeshi children live in the most deprived areas, for example, obviously correlating with their lower attainment. This therefore does not appear to be an ethnic issue.

However the vast array of data sampled here is sliced, substantial gaps of varying sorts are clear. Their differing sizes are not important to the key arguments of this book. Some of these are clearly related to the family, community, material circumstances and other experiences referred to earlier, and are nested in the social and economic inequalities discussed in the last section. Whatever its limitations, the Feinstein 2003/DCSF 2009b graph does show that these differences may well be apparent long before school.

The relative contribution of schooling

But a proportion of the gaps, certainly by the age of 16, may be attributable to what happens *in* school, and this is the point of considering it against the background of such social and economic inequality. Rasbash *et al.* (2010) attempt to apportion the gap between the 'pupil characteristics' – what they bring into school with them – on the one hand, and what schools can change, on the other. Their apportionment is that the school can make up to about 22 per cent difference in attainment: attending a school designated as outstanding (by the English inspection agency Ofsted) is important. 'About' is significant, as the nature of these gaps varies and there is a complicated intersectionality in schools between ethnicity, gender and social class (Strand, 2014a; Strand, 2014b).

In addition to the social attainment gradient being much steeper in England than in other countries, it differs by ethnic group. For example, for white British pupils, the gradient affects the progress they make as well as attainment – thus broadening the attainment gap by the age of 11, and again at 16 (*ibid.*), as the Social Mobility and Child Poverty Commission also aver (2014), though white boys are outperformed at higher levels of socio-economic status by those from Indian backgrounds. And white children overall make less progress at secondary level than all other ethnic groups. For black Caribbean boys, however, there is little social class advantage in the progress they make, signifying a substantial level of underachievement at 16 compared to all other ethnic groups that cannot be accounted for just by their socio-economic status. This chimes to an extent with the findings of the 'black middle-class project' (see, for example, Vincent *et al.*, 2013) that examined some of the social processes involved. Importantly, however, Strand points out that for 16-year-olds, as a consequence (2014b), while the achievement gap by social class was twice as large as that for the biggest ethnic one, and six times as large as that for gender, this does not provide the overall explanation.

Can schools close these gaps? And if so, how?

In his consideration of the intersectionality at primary school, based on work in one London borough, Strand identifies that the school effect in outcomes for 11-year-olds, after adjusting for prior attainment and background, had 'no differential effect on entitlement to free school meals, gender or ethnic background' (Strand, 2014a: 40). In other words, the more effective schools, while raising the achievement of disadvantaged children, have also raised that of the advantaged. Therefore, at least historically, they have not been able to narrow this gap, he argues, and he found the same result in an earlier analysis of all 14,500 primary schools in England (Strand, 2010).

In Strand's complex, secondary whole-cohort analysis (2014b), he begins to identify and measure a range of the factors that might affect differential attainment and progress. These include aspects of parents' attitudes and behaviour, such as their aspirations (see Gregg and Goodman, 2010, for a separate consideration of their effects), monitoring progress (see also Lareau, 2000, for an account at elementary school level in the United States), providing a computer, and offering extra tuition. All of these appear to be significant. Compare this list with that of Holloway *et al.* (2014). It also reflects Sylva *et al.*'s (2010) considerations of what they termed the 'home learning environment' (HLE) (see a good summary on pages 60–2), which they further investigated in working-class and ethnic minority homes (Siraj-Blatchford, 2010).

Strand further considers what he terms the 'pupil risk' factors for these differential outcomes (summarized at 2014: 158): whether homework is actually *done*, having special educational needs, experiencing exclusion, not attending school and having varying attitudes to school. Measuring these pupil and family factors, together with those identified by the EPPSE Team (Sylva *et al.*, 2010) for the early years and the broader range of resources and other factors that enable the transmission of advantage or disadvantage across generations (Feinstein *et al.*, 2008), enables us to build a broader and more detailed picture of the limiting mechanisms of social reproduction (Bourdieu and Passeron, 1977) in England, in and out of schooling.

Such identifications are the starting points for policy. If we know and understand how these social and other mechanisms are working, interventions can be developed to counter them – if we are really committed to widening participation and increasing social mobility, as most UK politicians are (Riddell, 2013) – rather than keeping children in their place through IQism. These interventions may be national, local, regional or all three. Answering the '*what* is going on?' question from these outcome data, however, may not tell us the 'how' or the 'why' in the complexities of the communities schools serve. Kintrea *et al.*'s (2011) analysis for the Joseph Rowntree Foundation of three very different UK working-class communities is but one of many studies that suggest there cannot be one simple straightforward intervention that will work everywhere.

Further, although children's lives are embedded or nested in a much wider range of family and community experiences and interpretations than those they have in school, schools do attempt to influence the factors mentioned by Strand rather than remaining hermetically sealed off from the communities they serve. They do try to work on social structure. Strand calls for 'more nuanced accounts of educational success or failure' (2014b: 165), which are clearly needed, and schools in turn require – need to shape – nuanced responses, which may vary over time as well as place, particularly in the context of global migration.

And again, although Strand demonstrated in his earlier study (2010) that better schools raised the achievement for *all* children evenly rather than narrowing the gaps for those who were disadvantaged, this does not mean that this *cannot* be done. Whitty and Anders' (2013) commanding and detailed study examines what changed under the Labour Government during the first ten years of the twenty-first century; they argue that the Coalition Government (2010–15) had a more ambitious commitment to 'closing' rather than 'narrowing' the attainment 'gap' (as noted by the National Audit Office) between disadvantaged students and those without disadvantage. Nevertheless, in contrast to the attainment data reported in DfE (2014a; DfE, 2014d), Whitty and Anders point to a 'steady weakening of the overall correlation between household deprivation and educational performance in the years between 2006 and 2010' (Whitty and Anders, *ibid*: 15) under the Labour Government. Specifically, they say later (*ibid*: 29), drawing on the official review of the City Challenge initiative, begun in London (Hutchings *et al.*, 2012), there is evidence that both the number of underperforming schools was reduced *and* the performance of students entitled to free school meals was raised, faster than the national average.

These particular policy formations are considered in detail in Chapters 3 and 4. They do point to the *possibility* of disadvantaged students succeeding, and what might be done more broadly. However, none of this is done in the circumstances of our own choosing, as Marx reminds us. The school improvement programme launched by Labour in 2003 – the London Challenge and later the City Challenges (Riddell, 2003) – very much constituted a policy creature of the time, framed around the notions of 'deliverology' (Barber, 2008). Through the Challenges, discussed further in Chapter 3, direct connections were made between specific central government officials and those responsible for delivering key targets. There are still elements of that, but the Prime Minister made it clear early on in the life of the Coalition Government (Cameron, 2010) that he thought schools were better placed pleasing parents than the DfE – a stance on which the Government might since not have acted (see Chapter 7) – but in the meantime there has been major strategic change in the polity which makes for different policy possibilities.

What this book is not

The book does not attempt to construct in detail the ideal policy or polity that will work for disadvantaged students, divorced from the context in which English schools work, but it does begin to examine the possibilities that may emerge. There is much engaging – what I would term utopian writing; beside Coffield and Williamson (2011), there is, for example, Barker (2010), and Fielding and Moss (2011). These are inspiring books that help us (and our students) focus on the sort of world and education service we would like to have. All these books reward time spent on them, and it is not possible to do full justice to them here. Indeed, Barker's book inspired a whole journal issue (*Journal of Educational Administration and History*, 2011, Volume 44, issue 1).

Barker analysed what he terms the 'five illusions' of school reform (Barker, 2010: 4 onwards) and painted a powerful vision of recovering 'progressive' principles (in many ways rooted in experience I share of comprehensive school teaching), committed to a new vision of empowering children on the basis of their own and community values to build democracy. His implicit message is that 'top-down reform', the motor of the deliverology-based bureaucratic state, makes this impossible, distorting teaching into teaching-to-the-test. Aspects of this are reflected in the following pages.

In their advocacy of radical education through the common school, Fielding and Moss similarly write about creating and recreating a democratic society rooted in schools with autonomous teachers and learners. They advocate a critical pedagogy in a long tradition (see Dardar *et al.*, 2009) in which schools link with local marginalized and oppressed communities. They call for measures to counter the hollowing out of the individual they maintain has been the result of neoliberalism whereby consumers are created with a set of acquisitive choice preferences rather than deeper beliefs about the good life and how all should be able to access it. The provision of democratic education requires the (re)construction of schools attended by all the children in the communities they serve – this was the original vision many of us had when entering teaching in the 1960s and 1970s. Finally, Coffield and Williamson's (2011) similar advocacy of a more 'democratic professionalism', and radical change 'from the very roots upwards' (*ibid*: 34), describe the demoralizing effects of a national testing regime which, together with the market, has made inequalities worse. Again, you will see elements of this in this book.

I do not disagree with these prognoses. I have argued myself (Riddell, 2003) that the stratification of school systems has been made worse by a combination of marketization reforms and a newer and developing middle-class agency in the education market (see also Ball, 2003). The focus on performance and its continuing effects on teachers and students have real and sometimes negative consequences, distorting what many teachers would like to be doing. A record number of teachers (50,000) left the profession in 2014 (Morrison, 2015), some at least as a result of the introduction of various Coalition Government reforms, many of which are discussed in this book. This needs to change.

But such writing does not tell the whole story. Advocating what would inevitably be, as all these authors say, radical changes that bear little relation to the current organization of schooling in England leaves questions about what to do now open and unanswered. These are the sort of 'what shall we do on Monday afternoon?' questions that Apple (2012) and others wrestle with: is it possible to 'resist', as he says, now, the (limited) expectations that our society has of many of its children, and be ambitious for them? He says it is. In the book he wrote jointly with James Beane, *Democratic Schools* (2007), the authors document precisely this sort of resistance that avoids leaving young people bereft of direction in a neoliberal world.

Inequity did not start, however, with neoliberal reform or the marketization of public services. It is rooted in our society; the accompanying economic changes of the past forty years have just worsened it. Although, classically, those born in 1958 had greater social mobility – or 'opportunity to better themselves' – than those born in 1970 (Blanden *et al.*, 2005; Milburn, 2009), the changes were not due to the schooling they received, but to changes in the occupational structure of society, in the opportunities available (Bottero, 2005), and constituted no more than what Goldthorpe (2007) would consider *structural* mobility or change. Society had become no fairer, no more encouraging to those from disadvantaged backgrounds. There was just a different pattern of jobs available that needed to be filled.

I would say with regret that such accounts do not offer any answers to the inequities in attainment outcomes for the young people going through our schools today or the structuring accompaniment these represent to their social, educational and occupational trajectories. Nor do the authors actually admit that *some* of this is due to what actually happens *in* schools. So, although this book returns in Chapter 7 to the issues of wider social and economic policy, and whether the background reality documented here can be changed, it focuses chiefly on what schools – teachers and heads – can do and are doing *now* to potentially make people's lives better.

Although the visions of Barker and others are inspiring, the investigation described in this book focuses on the system-in-development and what it makes possible from where we are *at this juncture*. Whether change is illusory, as Barker in particular would seem to argue, or not, I treat this as an empirical question: what can be done now? Even so, the logic of a developed self-improving schools system could indeed see many aspects of Barker's, Fielding's, Moss's, Coffield's and Williamson's visions eventually realized.

Chapter 2

Getting to 'Good': Investigating a system-in-development

I think our future, hopefully ... is in our own hands now. And so we are looking ... to kind of mould our own future really, based on what we believe to be right for [our school] – right for the youngsters in the area and right for the future of education. Now, with the LA diminishing and having been offered all sorts of support, we can choose the partners we work with.

(Martin, secondary headteacher,
maintained school, metropolitan area)

[The decline in LAs] had a major influence on me, because ... you did feel that all the sticks were being thrown up in the air and 'let's just see where they land'. And nothing's gone against that for me since, because every time different bits of information are dripped through, you're not completely clear; there aren't any definite rules. Like if a school goes into a[n Ofsted] category, the head automatically goes. Well in many cases they do. And colleagues of mine who I've been in touch with suddenly aren't in touch any more and don't give you any explanation as to what happened to their school.

(Arthur, primary headteacher,
maintained school, shire county)

Background

The research for this book began with an investigation into the differing approaches being taken to social mobility policy either side of the 2010 UK general election. This followed on from my earlier consideration of aspiration-forming as a classed social process (Riddell, 2010), seen then in policymaking terms as a possible motor for increasing mobility, though with little apparent backing from research (Gorard *et al.*, 2012). The findings at that time (Riddell, 2013) indicated that politicians of all political persuasions had made similar commitments towards increasing mobility and widening opportunity, but the 2010–15 Coalition Government had begun to consider the role of the state differently as far as the *realization* of policy (after Trevor Gale, 2003) was concerned. The term *realization* is preferred to *implementation* because it represents more realistically the complex processes that occur between stating education policy intentionalities and seeing what happens to them when teachers try to carry them out with children. By the time of realization, policy details have been filtered through many different minds at different positions in the polity, all with differing experiences, conceptions, understandings and interpretations (Ball, 1990; Fullan, 2001). So the classroom realities for our seven and a half million children differ, irrespective of their other experiences.

Conservative politicians made public statements about the role of the state and state policy towards public services early in the Coalition Government's term. There was to be less bureaucratic top-down direction, less interference by central government officials in local services and more professional discretion (Cameron, 2010). These were reflected in early policy documents about education and schools. The White Paper published that year, *The Importance of Teaching,* made a clear statement about 'school responsibility' (DfE, 2010a: 5) for change, in itself by no means new or incorrect. But it also stated the Government's intention of 'making it easier for schools to learn from each other' and, in so doing, to 'support the school system to become more effectively improving' (*ibid*: 55). A '*self*-improving schools system' had become public policy, as I consider in detail in Chapters 3 and 4. The empirical focus of this book is on the extent and nature of the changes engendered by attempts to realize such a system and whether they are likely to provide a framework for addressing the equity issues rehearsed in Chapter 1.

What is apparent from the research for this book and for Riddell (2013) is that the English education system can no longer be characterized – if ever it could – by traditional descriptions of bureaucratic national policy development and local implementation, as David Cameron described them in his speech. The 'deliverology' model that Michael Barber (2008; 2011; 2015) continues to advocate, even in modified forms that replace delivery 'chains' with 'systems' (Riddell, 2013), never had but a narrow focus on a restricted number of priorities and no longer applies across all schools. The added complexities of English governance – the remaining role, if any, of the 'middle tier' (Crossley-Holland, 2012), the roles and relationships between professional leadership in schools and non-professional governing bodies – make it difficult in any case to find any single model of change, although one may be evolving.

The developing polity described over the next few chapters has already begun a radical process of replacing local democratic oversight with a service much more professionally supervised and led by headteachers (as argued by Hatcher, 2014). Individuals I interviewed at various stages for this research were enacting this policy (Ball *et al.*, 2012) particularly loyally – and surprisingly so in the case of some LAs and their officers – but many were also actively engaged in *shaping* local arrangements, including for the national and local arms of the Education State. Others were beginning to see the advantages to their work of the new evolving arrangements; Martin, the secondary headteacher quoted at the beginning of this chapter, was one of them. Others again, only marginally affected because of their own schools' outcomes for children and having achieved at least a 'good' judgement from Ofsted, were just beginning to understand the implications of these radical developments, not always comfortably, and how they might relate to them. Arthur, the primary headteacher quoted earlier, fell into this category. These different understandings of people in prominent positions in the polity demonstrate the current complexity and flux in its development.

At the same time, the complexity is increasing for other reasons. As part of the increasing diversification of initial teacher professional preparation (Carter, 2015), Teach First in particular has been bringing cohorts of people into state schools and schooling who were unlikely to have been involved before, following the Teach for America pattern. With the first Teach First graduates starting teaching in 2003, the 12 intervening years have allowed plenty of time for them to take their Leadership Master's qualifications and move into strategic and senior roles. Two such individuals were interviewed as part of this research, though they were not sought-out as such; more can be found in other positions. The two whom I interviewed were both dynamic and committed to reforming state schooling for disadvantaged children (a key aim of Teach First); both were thinking optimistically and strategically; and both were seeking to bring about radical change. This is a marker of the emergence in the polity of non-state actors (Ball and Junemann, 2012) such as the charity that runs Teach First. Both of those interviewed reminded me of the 'impatient optimists' strapline on the homepage of the Gates Foundation. Both represent the developing significance of 'philanthrocapitalism' (Bishop and Green, 2008) whereby public money is supplemented or replaced by private donations, for purposes not necessarily decided on democratically. Priorities selected and funded this way fit perfectly with a schools system that is professionally or purely headteacher-led.

But one word of caution: an ex-senior official who had worked directly for two Prime Ministers advised me when interviewed in 2012 to 'pay attention' to what Coalition politicians actually do, not 'just what they say'. The reality is that despite stated intentionalities, there still remain some very traditional command-and-control mechanisms for schools, as one interviewee described them, within which satisfying the requirements of national and regional organizations is the *sine qua non* of the continued working and sometimes very existence of schools and their leadership teams.

This adds further to the complexity and is consistent with Ball and Junemann's observation that the 'assemblages' of the developing nature of state education are unstable (2012: 138). There are different blends of 'steering and rowing' (*ibid*: 141) at work that in England, it is observed here, vary by location, status of school and the actors involved (as the two aforementioned heads I interviewed attest). With the election of a Conservative Government in 2015 this instability is likely to continue. But there is still much to play for.

The interview evidence base for this book

The arguments made in this book draw on primary evidence from three overlapping and connected series of new interviews, together in some cases with earlier interviews from other projects. These three distinct pieces of work are closely linked and, together, help illuminate the structural changes taking place in the polity the book describes.

The first series of interviews, in connection with social mobility strategies, was conducted between 2010 and 2012. It involved 22 people, mostly interviewed individually, but in two cases in groups. All except three of these interviews were conducted face-to-face, with two being conducted by telephone and one by an extended email exchange following initial telephone contact.

Interviewees included officials and ex-officials at Number 10, the Cabinet Office, the Department for Work and Pensions (DWP) and the Department for Business, Innovation and Skills (BIS). Individual officials were approached directly because of their advertised departmental lead responsibilities for social mobility. It did not prove possible to interview an official from the DfE at that time.

Interviews were also held with members of the Gateways to the Professions Collaborative Forum (see Riddell, 2013), chaired by the Minister of State at BIS. They were all senior members of their respective professional groups or associations (for example the Chartered Surveyors), suggested by officials, and responded positively to my approach. Other interviewees were either established in, or about to enter, the professions of medicine and engineering, from a widening participation perspective. The last of this series of interviews was conducted in early 2012.

The second series of interviews commenced in 2013 and covered 24 people who were in senior or strategically significant positions in the developing polity for schools. I began with three Directors of Children's

Services, sometimes accompanied by another responsible senior officer, in LAs of different types and sizes – one shire county, one unitary authority and one metropolitan borough in two English regions. This represented an opportunity sample, acquired through my own network. The Directors were asked to nominate at least two headteachers who might give differing accounts of the processes of change they were living through at the time. After consideration of these interviews, I approached other headteachers on an opportunity or snowballing basis.

As part of this second series I also interviewed senior and individual private sector providers of both consultancy and Ofsted inspections, the heads of three academy chains (one large and national, one medium-sized and regionally focused and one small local chain of two secondary and two primary schools). Interviews also took place with people involved in campaigning nationally or locally against academy conversion and, by way of contrast, those promoting free schools and supporting them once open.

One refrain from the initial stage of the second series of interviews (2013–14) – from headteachers, heads of academy chains and LA officers – concerned the background and perceived inconsistency of Ofsted Inspection Teams (much echoed in the *Times Educational Supplement* – see, for example, Stewart, 2014). As a consequence, I had further discussions with one of the Ofsted Inspection Service Providers, before school inspections were taken in-house with effect from 1 September, 2015. They revealed some disagreement with these reported views but also showed the wide range of backgrounds from which current additional inspectors, as they were then known, were drawn. This was confirmed by an examination of the web-based lists of additional inspectors of the two other private sector providers. The Inspection Service Provider agreed to carry a short text within selected emails advertising the wider research reported in this book and inviting contact from inspectors willing to contribute to it. Thirty offers were received almost by return.

Seventeen inspectors were interviewed over the 2014–15 academic year, largely by telephone but some face-to-face where travel was relatively easy. These inspectors came from a wide range of backgrounds, including serving and ex-primary, secondary and special headteachers, serving and ex-LA officers and various private sector roles. All were involved in development and support work with schools, in all phases and, even in the case of serving LA officers, on an individual contracted basis. They added another four LAs and three more regions including London to the research. Some interviewees were also working in the LAs already covered, giving helpfully complementary, and in some cases contrasting, views of developments. One interviewee later withdrew his data.

Overall, from the second and third phases of interviews, I interviewed 17 serving headteachers from across the country, though no one from further north than the West Midlands. At the time they were interviewed, the heads came from sponsored and 'converter', post-2010, academies (see Chapter 4), LA-maintained primary and secondary schools and an all-through free school (one interviewee). Their school Ofsted judgements were a mix of outstanding and good, with only one 'requiring improvement'. The significance of these Ofsted judgements for headteacher views are discussed later.

Some of these headteachers were representative, for example in being chair of the local primary heads' association, which added to the individuals' perspectives. The interviewees included two who have been appointed to new posts as Regional Schools Commissioners, thereby adding different insights to the development of the polity, although neither had taken up post at the time of interview.

Another face-to-face interview was conducted with a student at the University of what I refer to as 'Oxbridge' when I was reflecting on what it was like to be one of the 'brightest and the best', and on the role of schools in helping some young people achieve and (sometimes) assume this status.

Overall, I drew on 61 original live interviews in the writing of this book, excluding repeats and further email contacts. Headteacher interviewees will contribute to later research.

Conduct and focus of the interviews

I approached the interviewees in all three phases in writing, explaining the nature of the work of which the interviews were a part and the focus for possible questioning, which I dubbed the 'two-minute version' of the research. If an interview was agreed, either in person or by telephone, I sent a more detailed list of topics and questions a few days in advance. No one refused an interview, although in some cases it was not possible to arrange one at a mutually convenient time and one interviewee withdrew his data, as noted earlier. All were receptive to being interviewed and interested in the work and its follow-ups.

The first phase of interviews was concerned more with the Coalition's social mobility strategy (Cabinet Office, 2011) than the school-led system, so most discussions included the interviewees' roles and contribution to the strategy. I also asked the officials about the policy realization model and what they expected the role of schools to be. For the representatives of professional groups and some others, the interviews concerned their view of the national strategy and what difference it might make, including to people like themselves and those they might know in their respective associations.

The second and third series of interviews overlapped in timescale and content, all beginning with a focus on role and ending with an invitation to give a view on the wider developing system. There were other common themes: the changing role of LAs; the nature of school collaboration and whether it enabled joint practice involvement; their work with other schools if they were a national or local leader of education; the development of school and system capacity; their involvement with, and experiences of, Ofsted; and, for all, what motors there were in the developing system to keep senior leaders motivated and focused on improving children's attainment. Although questions were generic for the different groups, they were sometimes modified in the light of my developing knowledge of the local area. For example, in one LA this included the LA-supported development of school networks (Chapter 5). In any case, the generic headings correspond to those in government policy documents, reviewed in Chapter 4.

All interviews were therefore semi-structured, with prompts available to ensure data were comparable between interviewees. Topics were not always dealt with in the same order; I used my usual conversational interview style and open-ended questions ('Would you like to say something about ...?'), enabling the interviewees to follow their own logic while I ensured that all topics were covered.

The length of interviews in the first phase varied from one and a half hours for officials (two hours in one case) and professional organizations to about thirty minutes for the individual professionals. In the second phase, the standard requested length was an hour, which had to be strictly adhered to for many, but spread to two hours in some schools where I had a chance to look round and talk about broader topics and with teachers. For phase three, the interviews were between 40 and 90 minutes, the longer ones again being in schools.

All the interviews were recorded except one held in a coffee bar because no office space was available. Transcripts were professionally produced for all the interviews in the first and second phases with the help of small grants from my university. All interviewees were sent a copy of the transcript after a light edit and invited to offer any corrections, which some did, adding further comment. All direct quotations were sent for clearance with the individuals concerned. I also promised sight of any texts that drew on what they said, but all the arguments are my own. Some interviewees made further comments at this stage. In line with common practice and the ethics policy of my university, all were informed they could withdraw their data (only one did).

Given the nature of the interviews, the responses fell into several well-defined headings that will unfold in subsequent chapters. I began with some intuitive thematic coding, such as the importance of democracy in a public service, and then commenced some axial coding (Cohen, Manion and Morrison, 2010) to compare, for example, specific views on democracy among the LA officers' group, headteachers and others, but the views expressed were so similar that this was soon abandoned.

What these interviews represent and mean

I have had further contact with many of the interviewees since the original interview, some on a formal basis. Some had changed their minds on some topics in the intervening period – another marker of a system-in-development. But these interviews were not life history interviews; at best, as Goodson *et al.* say (2010), these are interpretations of lived experience at the time, but are nevertheless deeply rooted in professional experience. In her introduction to Bathmaker and Harnett (2010: 1), Bathmaker says, rightly, that policymakers use individual narrative vignettes to promote their causes, which is certainly the case for many policy documents drawn on for the present book, for example, DfE (2010a). So by the same token, the vignettes reported here of lived experience *illustrate* the actual process of change, or provide interpretive snapshots, which are just as 'real' (Riddell, 2010).

This is not just about making the link between personal troubles and public issues, as C. Wright Mills observed (cited in Bathmaker and Harnett, *ibid.*), although some of the interviews certainly did so. Because the well-positioned interviewees were mostly involved in shaping the new system, particularly in the second series, their reported experiences and concerns are also snapshots of the *system itself* as it is moving, developing and evolving. They illuminate government policy intentions as they move towards realization and thus allow a critical and deeper assessment to be made about whether the changes involved will help address the equity issues.

In addition, the virtue of making the private public (Bathmaker and Harnett, *ibid.*) in this way illustrates the complexity of national structural change: what might appear to be a simple idea of school-led change, albeit with many of its implications nationally unarticulated or possibly unconceived, passes too through many minds and interpretations before its realization can be characterized or understood. Policy evolves in complex ways, in my experience, rather than developing in simple linear patterns. It is probably impossible to say whether a system is finally in place or not – it certainly isn't yet according to Greany (2014). It will always remain an 'assemblage' (Ball and Junemann, 2012). This is probably the pattern of all polities in our society.

We must remain aware that interviewees, particularly at times of change, are actively constructing their own understanding and discursive knowledge of the change around the questions asked of them (Holstein and Gubrium, cited in Denzin and Lincoln, 2000) and therefore their articulation of the polity. This might not have happened without the interview. Moreover, it might affect their future actions. In addition to the interview data, discussed principally in Chapters 5 and 6, I found that very few of the interviewees in phase two and three had had an opportunity to discuss or think about the nature of the national changes in any depth with someone else – perhaps another indicator of the declining orbit of the LA. The development of their responses to the interview questions showed not only the construction of a narrative around the changes but also a professional thinking-through of the future implications.

Although I tried to gain a spread of views – professionally and geographically – the interview data reported here represents but a small sample of those involved in the current processes of change. Therefore, as the book moves towards judgement on the basis of the interview data and my critical reading of policy, I take great care to compare what emerges with other studies of the current changes in governance and school structures, particularly where these reflect different geographical areas, approaches or policy assumptions (for example, Simkins *et al.,* 2014; Boyask, 2015; Hatcher, 2014; and Crossley-Holland, various). So there is some attempt at triangulation (Denzin and Lincoln, 2000) with other studies that draw on interview data, enabling a more effective reading of policy (Ball, 1997) and the accounts of its realization. The significance of the data, then, can only be understood in the particular conjuncture of a change process that will continue for at least the next five years.

The stance of the author

Some consideration must also be given to my background and stance in gathering the interview data, as they may be seen to have coloured the data collected.

I have forty years' experience in and around state schools in England: as a teacher in comprehensive schools, an officer in four LAs, including seven as a Director of Education in a major English city, a consultant working with LAs and Local Skills Councils (now defunct) and, though less relevant to this research, as Head of Education for an international human rights NGO. This was before joining Bath Spa University over six years ago, where I have been teaching about education and schools to undergraduates who would largely become teachers and postgraduates studying at Master's or PhD level.

The recruitment of interviewees was fairly easy in that I could draw from an extensive professional network built up over a long career. This helped, for example, with identifying the precise official to speak to, who may not have been the one named in policy documents. Some of the interviewees were known to me professionally and some knew of me because of my previous roles, but the vast majority were not and did not. At the time, it was accepted by the interviewees that I had direct professional experience of their work contexts; in many cases this involved shared values that we did not explicitly question, such as commitment to challenging disadvantage and raising attainment. Instrumentally, I generally understood the parameters of their roles, without their having to spell them out.

So the interviews, although in many ways questioning current policy, did not challenge most of these values and working assumptions. Although both the values and assumptions may be regarded as the underpinning and infrastructure of neoliberal education policy – as they indeed are – I would argue that they also represent an attempt to explore what equity it is possible to achieve in the current circumstances that are not of our choosing, as Marx famously said in the *Eighteenth Brumaire* quotation. My own understanding of change in complex, social structures and formations, developed over many years of professional experience and more recently academic writing and research, is fluid, open and pragmatic, as one of my PhD examiners observed.

Further, my previous experience, particularly as an LA officer, has historically been based on additional values such as a deep belief in the democratic oversight of local public services. This belief was explicitly questioned and challenged in some of the interviews, while being wistfully recalled in others. All this is to say that I did not bring a blank sheet to the evaluation of the data: this experience and value-set arguably could not allow for a truly grounded approach (Glaser and Strauss, 1967), but then that might be impossible for anyone (Thomas and James, 2006). I did not welcome some of the findings reported here, but I believe we should continue to explore their implications while not representing everything current as a dystopia or, alternatively, building a fantastic utopia constructed without pupil testing.

It must be added that any regrets I might feel at the by now largely established demise of LA involvement in formal school improvement activities do not mean I see no role for the LA in schools. I discuss this in Chapters 6 and 7, particularly in relation to the effects of 'advanced forms of marginalization' (Kerr *et al.,* 2014: 34) on attainment, specifically in terms of what children bring into school. The LA is the only organization, leaving aside the impatient optimists of philanthrocapitalism, able to consider and legitimate what to do about marginalization systematically. As ever, this does not mean they will.

Finally, the initial questions for these interviews were very specific and could be said to have formed an initial view of the topic to which interviewees were asked to respond. This too would be correct, but the categories into which the questions fell are all set out in the Government's policy documents and help define the field for investigation. Whether that then determines action, or paints a full picture, is a matter for interpretation, but that does not prevent the responses from providing a ready interpretation of government intentionality and the current state of its realization – and, importantly, non-realization. They still represent the 'lived reality' of the reform and show how these senior post-holders are positioned within it (Gunter, 2012).

So for the purposes of this book, the triangulated reasonable consensus areas from the interviews are taken as adumbrating the principal features of the polity, as set out in policy documentation, as it changes and is lived now. This adumbration, triangulated with other studies, forms the basis of my analysis of the potential realization of equity that follows.

Please note I have given pseudonyms to interviewees I refer to frequently over the next few chapters to avoid having to introduce them each time. In the listing at the beginning of the book I provide a little more detail on the positions they held, consistent with preserving anonymity. At the same time, commentators at various stages of the writing process of this book have pointed out the growing complexity in the lexicography of the emerging polity. I have therefore added a glossary of terms (also at the beginning of the book) that I hope readers will find helpful.

Chapter 3

Ratcheting up the expectations on schools: Changing policy frameworks

Primary Schools in England are getting better, but improvement in secondary schools has stalled. Eighty-two per cent of primary schools are now good or outstanding, which is an increase of three percentage points over last year. By contrast, just 71 per cent of secondary schools are at least good, a figure that has not changed since 2012/13. The proportion of pupils doing well in the national tests at the age of 11 has risen by three percentage points this year. In comparison, GCSE results have not risen over the last three years and the gap in attainment at GCSE between pupils from poorer backgrounds and their more affluent peers is not closing quickly enough.

(Ofsted, 2014b: 4)

So I've put my own leadership team in there and we have a plan to improve the school … The improvement plan looks like many of our improvement plans, which is … fundamentally focused around attendance, behaviour, teaching and learning, data tracing and monitoring. It's not meant to be clever or visionary, it's meant to be really pragmatic, to do the job … and while there will be some innovative stuff wrapped up in that, fundamentally [the school] doesn't have the capacity to be innovative right now, it just needs to be good at the normal stuff.

(Daniel, head of academy chain)

A potted history of neoliberal education policy

The policy intention of a school-led, self-improving system and its formation, I argue, can only be understood if located within the language and history of what Harvey (2011) describes as the neoliberal policy turn. In this chapter I take such an approach, up until about 2010, drawing on key policy documentation, academic analyses and my own professional experience as a senior officer in LAs for a major part of the period under discussion.

Although neoliberal education policy formations in England and elsewhere have been evolving for nearly forty years, this has not been a straightforward linear development process because of the wider social, cultural and political processes of which they form part. Particular aspects of policy acquire greater or lesser significance at different times. Some of those relevant to the evolution of a school-led system are picked out here.

Chronologically, the beginning of the development of neoliberal policy for English schools is often dated to the speech made at Ruskin College, Oxford, in 1976 by the UK Prime Minister James Callaghan (Barber, 1996; McCulloch, 2001). Callaghan spoke of higher standards and expectations on schools, the 'methods and aims' of instruction, monitoring to set national standards, the possibility of a core curriculum and the role of the Inspectorate (Barber, *ibid*: 34).

What developed subsequently in England was similar to that elsewhere. Whitty *et al.* noted common developing features of schools policy in five Western industrialized countries (Whitty *et al.*, 1998: 9), four of them English-speaking including England, and there were related features in policy developments in other countries. In 2002, Whitty observed the commonalities between the respective policies of the UK Labour Government, then five years old, and the previous Conservative one from 1979 to 1997.

Later in the decade, the schools systems reports from the McKinsey Global Initiative (McKinsey, 2007; 2010) were framed entirely within the same neoliberal assumptions about the need to drive up school performance. McKinsey identified the characteristics of school systems they judged to be successful in doing so. The neoliberal enterprise had become truly international.

Both the Conservative and the Labour parties cited the first of these reports (McKinsey, 2007) as authority for their policy proposals for the 2010 UK General Election campaign, while drawing on the most recent results of the Programme of International Student Assessment (PISA) (OECD, 2010). The first Education White Paper of the UK Coalition Government, *The Importance of Teaching* (DfE, 2010a) did similar. This continues.

There were other policy continuities on either side of the 2010 election too, for example, in social mobility policy and strategy (Riddell, 2013) and there is a clearly identifiable, common international intentionality and framework for national *social* policy. Mirowski (2013), while writing primarily about the unchanging nature of neoliberal economic theory, in spite of the 'Great Recession' of 2007–8, makes the point that, historically, neoliberalism appears to survive the deepest crisis, more or less unmolested and, often, unchallenged within the policy community or anywhere else. This appears to be true in education as well.

So although there may be apparent differences, often emphasized, between Westminster UK political parties, the similarities are more real than apparent. Since Callaghan, all the main platforms of neoliberal education policy, with its focus on measurable and comparable outcomes for students and the market forces added later, have been justified in terms of what Lingard *et al.* refer to as 'economism' (1998), after Bourdieu. That is, the prime importance of education and its structures is in serving international economic competitiveness. Not only did this suffuse Callaghan's speech nearly 40 years ago, it is now also reflected in the rhetoric of international bodies such as the OECD (see Cingano, 2014, for example). The accompaniment to the Coalition Government's first Education White Paper (DfE 2010a), *The Case for Change* (DfE, 2010b), framed education reform in these precise terms. Wrigley refers to this 'economic rationalism' as 'reductionist' (2003: 25).

In England, the neoliberal policy framework for schools was established step by step during the 1980s and early 1990s. Parental choice was the first UK election pledge in 1979 and was enacted in 1982 following legislation two years earlier. This became known as 'open enrolment' in 1988, when schools were also given responsibility for their own delegated pupil number formula-driven budgets that enabled them to decide which support services they needed to buy in. External testing for children aged 7, 11 and 14 began, supplementing that for 16-year-olds, and published annually in 'performance tables'. A regular cycle of Ofsted inspections began in 1993 for secondary schools and 1994 for primary and special schools.

Ball characterized these reforms overall as 'competition, choice, devolution, managerialism and performativity' (2003: 30). Parental choice of accountable schools and teachers, it was intended, drawing on the annual performance tables (largely, still in 2015, based on raw attainment data), regular public school inspection reports and a national curriculum of sorts, would change school behaviour – and it did (Ball, 1994). In response to the competitive need and a financial one under the reforms to attract more children (parents), schools would up their game. They would improve the quality of their teaching and student attainment outcomes, the theory went, often in a very harsh public glare.

This public glare was framed by the shrill accompanying discourse of derision (Ball, 1994), alternatively referred to as a crisis account (Gorard, 2000) or narrative (Riddell, 2003), focusing on some or many schools. This discourse has since almost entirely constituted the terms in which schools are discussed in the media, by parents and communities and, eventually, everyone else, with some honourable exceptions in universities (see Wrigley *et al.*, 2012). That schools and teachers needed to become more accountable, therefore, reflected in Le Grand's classic description as potential public service 'knaves' (1997; 2003), became difficult to reconcile with trusting teachers or public servants more widely (Le Grand's 'knights') as had been done in the previous 'golden age'. Schools and teachers became market *players*.

Taken together, these reforms constitute one of Ball and Junemann's policy 'assemblages' (2012) that remains unstable. Within a constant overall process of neoliberal policy formation, government intentionality and action (which may themselves be different) vary. David Blunkett, the first Secretary of State for Education (and Employment) in the Labour Government (1997–2001), said he thought the teaching profession had been 'crap' before Labour took office in 1997, though it was not so any more. He was addressing a House of Commons Committee in 2010 (Bangs *et al.*, 2011). He had intended to do something about it, and indeed he did, but not just by relying on the market and parent consumers. The strict accountability and delivery lines that were developed across central government are what later became known as Michael Barber's 'deliverology' (2008; 2015). Barber was adviser to Blunkett from 1997–2001 and then to Tony Blair from 2001–5.

In complete contrast, the significant speech made by the Prime Minister early on in the Coalition Government (Cameron, 2010) could be seen as being at the other end of the spectrum of intentionality within the same neoliberal assumptions. His view was echoed by most Conservative members of his Cabinet, according to one of his officials I interviewed. They thought parents should have more effective mechanisms to hold schools to account before deciding to move their children elsewhere. The Coalition Government's commitment to transparency (Cabinet Office, 2011) led to much more data appearing on the DfE website (now through gov.uk), making comparison between schools easier. Ofsted's 'Parent View' now allows parents to post comments about their children's schools, triggering additional inspections if deemed necessary.

Moreover, some of these politicians, according to the official, thought that should be the end of it – parents got the schools for their children they deserved. If schools remained poor and parents did nothing, then that was down to them. And there were arguments in the House of Commons during the passage of the Health Bill – that was to reform the entire commissioning arrangements for the National Health Service (Pollock and Price, 2013) – about whether the Secretary of State for Heath should have *any* general responsibility in law to secure a health service in the future. But the various incumbents of the post continued to intervene in hospital trusts, just as their Education counterpart enforced academy conversions on sometimes unwilling schools (Riddell, 2013).

So these were shifts within a neoliberal assemblage; there are others. The publication of detailed performance data for the first time beyond some of those for 16-year-olds from 1988 provides a backdrop to these shifts. The increasing sophistication of the data demonstrated widespread differences between schools, beyond those related to the social and ethnic backgrounds of students. This, together with 'naming and shaming' poor performers (Bangs *et al.*, 2011), fed and reinforced the media's crisis narrative (Riddell, 2003) about left-wing 'progressive' teachers, and the 'worst schools' in the country, often in urban areas (O'Connor *et al.*, 1998). Some schools had dropped into the roles of Le Grand's 'knaves' and, ably abetted by those of us who worked in universities or LAs, were easily identified as part of what came to be referred to more recently and pejoratively as the 'Blob' (Young, 2014).

A taste for improving schools by central government

Whatever the varying public emphasis on the market, I maintain, intervention has always been an important aspect of Government policy. The shifts in the assemblage have been about who should intervene in schools and when, how and to what extent. The history of intervention is, paradoxically, the policy background to the developing notion of a school-led system.

In one sense, the idea of intervention is natural enough. Parents dismayed by the apparent poor performance of their local school or LA, the argument goes, may want to see them improved rather than their having to do it themselves or use the market mechanisms to opt for more distant schools, though many have done just this for over thirty years. If the profession is or was indeed 'crap', as Blunkett said, the citizen-consumer (Whitty, 2002) would expect some agency of the state to do something about it.

One of the significant developments from the mid-1990s onwards was the co-option by central government of the twin research 'movements' (Slee *et al.*, 1998) of School Effectiveness and School Improvement. Formally, this began with a letter written on behalf of the Conservative Secretary of State, Gillian Shepherd, to all Chief Education Officers of LAs entitled *Improving Schools* (DfE, 1995). The differences between the research movements, or traditions or paradigms as others term them, will not be laboured here, but the search for the characteristics of effective schools (judged by outcomes – again) had its beginnings in the 1970s with the *Rutter Report* (Rutter *et al.*, 1979), which attempted to counter earlier views that schools cannot make a difference (Coleman *et al.*, 1966). Efforts began in earnest in the 1980s: see for example Teddlie and Stringfield (1993), reporting on a ten-year project in Louisiana, and Sammons *et al.* (1995) for a summary of the research for England, published jointly by Ofsted at that stage. This led to a consideration of whether these characteristics could be developed in, or transplanted into, *ineffective* schools, thus curing them. Politically led and motivated school improvement programmes had begun.

There followed a ten-year period of increasing prescription. The Gillian Shepherd letter announced a 'tough and comprehensive programme of measures to raise standards' (page 1 of the accompanying press release, summarizing a key public crisis refrain). The programme included funding to help schools just inspected to develop and implement post-Ofsted plans, and urged all schools to address their identified priorities for improvement and set improvement targets. There have been many accounts of this period of policy, including my own of the first part of it (Riddell, 2003), but see Bangs *et al.* (2011). Policy was based on a consensus of sorts, but not an academic one (see Tomlinson, 1998 in the Slee *et al.* collection).

The national literacy and numeracy pilot projects began in LAs during 1996–7, supported by the Education Support Grant Funding promised in the Gillian Shepherd letter, and were accompanied by the publication by Ofsted of Reynolds' and Farrell's 1996 landmark *Worlds Apart*. In it, animated by the economism narrative, the favoured pedagogies of successful, specifically Pacific Rim, countries – based on whole (large) group interactive teaching (Whitty, 2002) – were identified and advocated. Following the appointment of 'task groups' on either side of the 1997 election, the primary literacy (1998) and numeracy (1999) strategies commenced, based on a version of Reynolds' and Farrell's book (Reynolds was on the numeracy task group). Primary schools were told in great detail not only how each of their lessons should be organized and delivered, but what the content should be at each stage, week and day. The Key Stage 3 Strategy (11–14-year-olds) was implemented in 2001 and 2002, based on a similar pedagogical model, the three or four-part lesson.

From 1999 onwards, attainment targets were set, beginning with national targets for 11-year-olds in English and Mathematics (literacy and numeracy). These were duly translated down, through a methodology not publicized at the time, into targets for LAs – given out in brown envelopes at an event in Westminster Hall – and thence to schools. Schools received notional targets from their LAs derived from ever-richer pupil data provided by Ofsted and LA data teams, but the responsibility was accepted to be theirs. Thus began the process whereby the contribution made by individual children to school targets for improvement could be identified and, hence, their progress in-year tracked towards them. Thus began too the data-gathering and -driven transformation of the teaching profession in

England. The first national arrangements for the performance management of teachers, whose salary progression could depend on their pupils' specified progress, were implemented from 2001 (DfEE, 1998).

All these changes were announced in the first Labour Education White Paper, *Excellence in Schools,* published within months of the 1997 General Election (DfEE, 1997). They are fully discussed in Riddell (2003). The model was such that, not only were schools *able* to improve, they were responsible for doing so. They should be encouraged by a combination of 'pressure and support', a phrase much used at the time, including in the White Paper. The knaves in schools could thus become knights by adopting methods for improving themselves, based on best evidence.

The model for improvement outlined in the subsequent White Paper, however, for the Blair Government's second term, *Schools Achieving Success* (DfEE, 2001), was now described as '*high* challenge, *high* support'. Ambitious targets were to be set and translated down to class and individual pupil level, it was intended, drawing on Ofsted data and evidence of best practice, including from government-sponsored training for literacy and numeracy. Schools were expected to achieve them, additionally held to account by more regular inspection visits and the continuing annually published performance tables. Should a school nonetheless fail, it was argued, it could expect intervention (Riddell, 2003: 122). This scenario became increasingly frequent.

The developing taste for intervention

The LA would make the intervention, often beginning with the withdrawal of the school governing body's powers to spend its delegated budget and therefore appoint or dismiss staff. When Ofsted deemed a school to be 'inadequate' and require 'special measures', an 'Interim Executive Board' (DCSF, 2008) could later be appointed to replace the governing body and oversee the development of the school. Individuals were handpicked by the LA to hold senior staff to account, by 'performance managing' them as it became termed.

After intervention, a new headteacher or principal would generally take up post, sometimes on a time-limited basis. By the third Labour White Paper (DfES, 2005a: 36), LAs were being advised, where necessary, to make an 'immediate change of headteacher' who would be expected to bring a new senior team with them, in whole or part. Leadership was becoming seen as the principal lever for improvement, soon to be termed transformation (Barker, 2010). School leaders were increasingly positioned as the crucial implementers of continuing national reform, as Gunter (2012) demonstrates – which they were. This is the historical background to the views about leadership expressed in the Ofsted annual report of 2014 – 'strong leadership is crucial but not enough schools have good leaders' (2014b: 4) – quoted at the top of this chapter.

School development or improvement plans, a Conservative Government reform, became central to this process. Under Labour they became an expectation and then a requirement (DfEE, 1997). An improvement plan after a poor Ofsted verdict was meant to focus on the weaknesses identified by the inspection, be they related to attainment, the quality of teaching, attendance or ineffective leadership – much as described by Daniel at the beginning of this chapter. Such a plan would put into place mechanisms such as lesson observation, training, mentoring and target-setting. Importantly, identifiable and measurable changes in performance were expected after 12 months, with the school providing an 'acceptable' standard of education – marking the end of special measures – after two years (Ofsted, 1997; 1999; 2001). The focus increasingly appeared, however, to be on the first year (DfES, 2005).

The discourse everywhere became about 'underachievement' (DfEE, 1997) and 'tackling school failure' (Ofsted, 1997). This developed into 'raising standards further' (Ofsted, 2001) and, later, 'transformation', as noted. Transformation appeared in the title of the Secondary Strategy, that incorporated the Key Stage 3 Strategy (DfES, 2002), and in that of a short pamphlet written by the Secretary of State (Blunkett, 2000). These crisis terms cannot be easily reconciled with the notions of steady improvement, perhaps with a new head or other staff brought in, inherent in much of the earlier school improvement research with its emphasis on addressing the internal conditions for learning in schools (Gray *et al.*, 1999). And, as national strategies for tackling under-achievement developed, strategies for 'Schools Facing Challenging Circumstances' (Hopkins *et al.*, 2001), or 'Exceptionally Challenging Circumstances' (Harris *et al.*, 2006), or merely those 'in difficulty' (Clarke, 2005), accompanied them, leading to the National Challenge policy (DCSF, 2008). By now, a change in schools' legal status had become one of the externally imposed and nationally favoured improvement measures.

Originally, this began with the so-called 'fresh start' and, at the extremes, Education Associations (see Stoll and Myers, 1998, and O'Connor *et al.*, for early accounts), whereby the school became a new legal entity overnight. This enabled many schools to dismiss staff, and it became something of a norm. As a by-product, the permanent exclusion of large numbers of children was agreed. Fresh start schools retained their community or other status, overseen by the LA. But when academies, originally city academies, began to open in 2002, the relationship with the LA began to fracture. 'Floor targets' were developed for struggling secondary schools (DCSF, 2007), as part of the national strategies, and have increased almost annually from the original 15 per cent GCSEs at 5A*–Cs in 2003, to 50 per cent in 2015 (DfE, 2010) and now 60 per cent.

A quick-intervention response became explicit in the national narratives – where it remains – leaving aside who or what had been watching the schools before intervention was seen to be needed. By the time the National Challenge policy was announced under the Gordon Brown Government, intervention could be triggered just by failure to achieve the floor targets. Furthermore, although it was intended to be facilitated by LAs, a change of leadership (still) and change of status to academies (more so now) or trusts became the first option (Riddell, 2009).

The declining role of LAs in school improvement

LAs, or local education authorities (LEAs) as they were known until 2002, were – on and off – honoured partners of central government in the school improvement process, but no more than that, particularly after the Gillian Shepherd announcements (DfE, 1995). Following the inception of Ofsted inspections in 1993, many LAs had made redundant sometimes large numbers of curriculum and leadership staff who had worked directly with schools. They were often termed 'advisers' or 'inspectors', as opposed to the staff of children's services such as welfare officers or special educational needs teachers. And since 1989, after parental ballots, schools had been allowed to 'opt out' of their LA by achieving grant-maintained status. In some parts of the country, many began to do so (Fitz *et al.*, 1993).

Under the subsequent Labour Government, and under the provisions of the *Excellence in Schools* White Paper (DfEE, 1997), LAs had to produce their own education development plans, setting out how they would work with schools to raise their pupils' attainment in accordance with an agreed, much-discussed national Code of Practice (Riddell, 2003). The LA staff that were left thus became involved in the target-setting processes, developing the school improvement plan, advising on senior and other appointments where a school governing body wished it and then advising on their performance management. Varying portions of this work were charged for, allowing schools to seek advice and support elsewhere if they wished. LAs also hosted the (centrally managed) staff and major national training programmes associated with the three national strategies that later became two – primary and secondary. Grant-maintained schools were, sort of, returned to LAs as foundation schools by 1999, albeit with few of their independent powers altered.

Ofsted began inspections of LAs from 1997 and required them to produce their own improvement plans following the identification of any weaknesses, including failure to intervene adequately in underperforming schools. Those receiving severe judgements in turn received intervention themselves, often through the private sector, but not always successfully, beginning with Hackney in 1998 (*ibid.*). These interventions continue.

Academies were originally conceived as an intervention into 'seriously failing schools' in deprived areas (Blunkett, 2000: 2) – hence the 'city' in the original title. Some schools sought this status for other reasons, including the greater likelihood (in the early days) of significant capital development and involvement with a sponsor. With their increasing numbers, academies began to represent a more significant change and challenge for LAs (Academies Commission, 2013). Academies' relationships became much more focused on central rather than local government. They had a funding agreement with the Secretary of State that entailed supervision from what became known as the Education Funding Agency, a body continuing at the time of writing in 2015 with just under 200 civil servants.

By the time the Coalition Government took power in 2010, this change became strategic with the huge expansion of academies (Academies Commission, 2013; Simkins, 2015) and was accompanied by other changes that had been progressively developing for over ten years. *Higher Standards, Better Schools for All*, the third Labour White Paper (DfES, 2005a), had been significant first in signalling the desirability for *every* school of acquiring a trust governance structure, similar to that for academies.

These changes of governance instituted in 2005 remained at the 'heart of the system' after the 2010 election. A new national Schools Commissioner had been appointed to 'drive change' (*ibid*: 8). National Leaders of Education (NLEs), later also Local Leaders (LLEs), and later still, Specialist Leaders (SLEs), were to be accredited by the National College for School Leadership which in 2005 was said, itself, to be under 'powerful new leadership'.

These significant 'system leadership' roles, defined as 'support[ing] the improvement of other schools as well as their own' (Hopkins and Higham, 2007: 147), have become important in the developing polity and are considered further in later chapters. LAs were now to become 'champions for parents and children in their area' (DfES, 2005a: 103). A 'new relationship' with schools (*ibid*: 109) was developing, originally signalled by the Minister for Schools in 2004 (Miliband, 2004) in a speech about personalized education. Although they were able to issue 'warning notices' to schools, LAs were now to focus on setting up collaborative arrangements to facilitate improvement, so 'good schools' would be able to 'take over other schools and spread their influence' (DfES, 2005a: 24) through so-called hard or soft federations. The later document *Education Improvement Partnerships* (DfES, 2005b) provided a framework for these procedures plus some funding.

Part of the 'new relationship' was the move away from the traditional work with schools undertaken by LA advisers or inspectors, increasingly now renamed School Improvement Advisers (SIAs) in line with the new national understandings. Schools were expected to contract with School Improvement Partners (SIPs), who were identified by LAs as part of the annual performance management arrangements for senior staff. These SIPs were to monitor, advise and challenge schools on their improvement and their strategies to address their weaknesses. It has been argued that they came into schools with a predetermined agenda (Bangs *et al.*, 2011). Some former advisers did become SIPs, but by the time of the National Challenge (DCSF, 2008) the clear expectation, at least for secondary schools, was that they would not. SIPs, now sometimes cast as Challenge advisers, were to be independent of LAs.

In the fourth and final Labour White Paper, *Your Child, Our Schools, Our Future* (DCSF, 2009a), the SIPs were given a wider role in *brokering* support, formerly a clear responsibility of LA staff. They were expected to ensure that 'challenging but achievable targets' (*ibid*: 80) were agreed by the school, and had to sign off improvement plans to reach these targets as a condition of the school's continuing central government grant. The LAs were expected to work through them. Their role as the champions for parents and children had developed into one of 'commissioning rather than providing education' (DfES, 2005: 103), providing data to schools and support for 'forming and maintaining partnerships'.

So LAs were now expected to be 'brokering local area clusters, National Challenge Trusts, partnerships, federations and, with the DCSF, academies' (DCSF, 2009a: 78). Some of these partnerships were to be with voluntary and private sector providers. The White Paper celebrated a partnership between Lincolnshire Council and the Centre for British Teachers (CfBT, a not-for-profit organization and, until 2015, an Inspection Service Provider) for the provision of school improvement services – a classic piece of neoliberal outsourcing. LAs were now 'clearly responsible' for 'ensuring maintained schools [were] effectively challenged'; note that this does not include academies, although this is not said directly. The

Secretary of State would also take the necessary steps should LAs not fulfil their responsibilities, largely via others or at arm's length.

This was the continually evolving and unstable assemblage affecting maintained schools inherited by the Coalition in 2010. LAs continued to lobby for having school improvement and intervention powers with respect to all state schools, including the hugely expanded numbers of academies after 2010 (see LGA, 2014a) as part of their roles as champions for all parents and children in their area. The DfE (as it again became in 2010), when later asked for formal clarification of the LA role in improving academies and free schools (specifically challenge), as part of the consultation on a government grant, made it absolutely clear in its response (DfE, 2014c) that LAs had no powers whatsoever over these schools. This met with much disappointment even though by then it was expected. But by this time, the creation of the regionalized central state for education was well under way and the LA was completely out of the picture regarding the governance of these schools.

Partnership working and the role of the LA

Finally, it is important to recognize that the notion of school partnerships was hardly new in 2005. It had been an important element of earlier reforms, albeit with a less strategic focus.

Education Action Zones, signalled in the DfEE White Paper of 1997, were targeted at groups of schools serving (mostly) uniformly deprived communities, often the size of a secondary school catchment area, and mirrored separate zones for health and employment. These groupings had a partnership governance arrangement, sometimes a board, a set of especially challenging attainment and attendance targets, and an action plan to achieve them within the lifetime of funding and their own staff – often a coordinator and sometimes others. Early on there were discussions about whether or not these supra-school bodies were part of the LA, but at the least these new staff supplemented LA staff and worked on collective Zone-based rather than LA priorities, which could cover a whole borough, city or county.

Views on their success were mixed (see for example Power *et al.*, 2005), and later Zones were incorporated, where possible, into the Excellence in Cities initiative which, from 2000, was intended to provide funding for six further compulsory initiatives (DfEE, 1999). These included collaborative programmes for gifted and talented students as well as those with challenging behaviour who needed time in area-based Learning Support Units – see Riddell (2003) and Kendall *et al.* (2005). Significantly, the initiative was to be overseen by a headteacher partnership board, to which LA officers were invited but elected politicians were not. In addition, the action plans to be submitted to the Secretary of State for these partnerships were to be agreed by the board, not the LA, despite its hosting the funding.

The London Challenge followed from 2003 (DfES, 2003), later incorporated into the wider City Challenge (DfES, 2007) in the Black Country (the English West Midlands) and Greater Manchester. All these areas had many smaller LAs, some of which had already accessed Excellence in Cities funding. All three Challenges promoted wider area-based school development and improvement. They had their own Challenge Advisers, sometimes part of the National Challenge, working with schools. There were common objectives, including reducing the number of underperforming schools. Priority was given to 'Keys to Success' schools in London and Manchester and 'Pathways to Achievement' schools in the Black Country. The aim was to increase the number of schools attaining 'Good' and 'Outstanding' Ofsted judgements and improve the educational outcomes for disadvantaged children overall.

From the beginning of the London Challenge, provision of individual pupil-level data was heavily emphasized so that teachers could plot progress carefully at classroom level. Initiatives across the three programmes differed, but all involved school pairings or triads, grouping schools into 'families' (often in different geographical locations but with similar profiles), all to share data. This, and the progress of each school, was the basis for examining the effectiveness of leadership (Hutchings *et al.*, 2012).

The emphasis, particularly in London, was on providing a bespoke and tailored programme, agreed between the (expert) Challenge Adviser and the school to address their specific needs, commonly in the use of data, for improving teaching and addressing leadership. For schools causing concern, this programme was reviewed annually at a triage meeting between central government officials, the LA and the Challenge Adviser (Hutchings *et al.*, 2012; Rudd *et al.*, 2011).

There were programmes for supporting teaching: the Outstanding Teacher Programme, the Improving Teacher Programme (which could be seen as early models of joint practice development – see Chapter 4) and professional development provided through new Teaching Schools. The increasing numbers of NLEs and LLEs (the system leaders) and subject consultants were deployed to work alongside school leaders. These programmes were implemented in parallel with national reforms such as the National Challenge and Teach First, absorbing some of them. Some structural changes in London were made to academy status, though these schools did not generally improve any faster than schools where no changes were made (Hutchings *et al.*, 2012). Overall, the programmes were seen by schools and teachers to be 'focused on support and challenge rather than blaming and shaming' (*ibid*: 39).

The role of the LA in these initiatives is interesting in as much as it presages the current polity. All three Challenges were supra-LA and involved 14 LAs in London, 10 in Manchester and 4 in the Black Country. Political leadership and support were provided *nationally* thorough ministerial teams, as Baars *et al.* (2014) point out, and in London five boroughs – Hackney, Southwark, Lambeth, Islington and Haringey – had themselves been singled out as Keys to Success (that is, poor performers), with all but Haringey receiving some sort of intervention. In contrast, Camden, Westminster and Tower Hamlets were seen to be high-performing.

Beyond the findings of Hutchings *et al.*, in a separate report Woods *et al.* (2013) analyse the huge improvements in attainment in the Borough of Tower Hamlets from the late 1990s. They argue that this was due to six major factors (*ibid*: 49), including strong local professional leadership and community involvement in a vision to improve, combined with a strong will to achieve it. Here again, though, the use of pupil data, partnership working and other similar work encouraged through the London Challenge were all highlighted.

LAs in London were encouraged by central government officials to collaborate with their neighbours in clusters to build capacity, undertake some joint work (just as schools were doing) and 'self-review' their school improvement work. Such work was less developed in the Black Country, but 'specific structured work' (Hutchings *et al.*, 2012: 94) was undertaken in some LAs perceived to be weaker, mentored by Challenge advisers. LAs did not always perceive this positively, they say, especially where the work began with the identification of weakness. But by the last year of the Challenges that coincided with the first year of the Coalition Government, Hutchings *et al.* report that many LAs were by then in any case dismantling their school improvement teams (*ibid.*) because of budget cuts. The data gathered for this book also show that many LAs were undertaking strategic reviews of their functions at about this time to accompany these cuts.

The strategic issue is that London, for example, was not treated as an LA-run system by the London Challenge: if the LAs were seen to be successful, they were worked *with* and sometimes *as part of* the strategy; if they were not, they were worked *on* through the supra-LA structure led elsewhere, involving central government officials and Challenge advisers who did not need or depend on LA boundaries.

The wider focus on equity and community

I have devoted space to the Challenges because they developed an infrastructure that was substantially, though not totally, intact at the beginning of the Coalition Government. Baars *et al.* (2014: 43) later raised the question of whether London itself could now be seen as a self-improving system, in line with Government expectations. These authors maintain that, as the provisions of the Challenge were accepted by both the first Secretary of State for Education under the Coalition Government, Michael Gove, and the second Mayor of London (2012), Coalition education policy as a whole could be viewed as an attempt to implement aspects of the London Challenge to scale (Baars *et al.*, 2014: 102). At the same time, there was the rapid increase in academies, now not needing to be seen as an intervention (Academies Commission, 2013; Simkins, 2015).

The observation of Baars *et al.* is relevant to the developing regional state, but only if the claims made for the London Challenge are true. The claim made by Hutchings *et al.*, echoed by Whitty and Anders (2013), that the London Challenge in particular had raised the attainment of deprived children in relation to others and had reduced the proportions of schools receiving poor Ofsted judgements, has been challenged more recently by Simon Burgess (2014). He argues that, statistically, the attainment gains made by London schools are attributable to their differing ethnic composition with differing cultural commitments to educational attainment. What are minorities outside London, he argues, are majorities inside. This to an extent echoes the findings of Kintrea *et al.* (2011).

Baars *et al.* examined three aspects of what they term 'the London Advantage' (2014: 44 onwards): gentrification (the social transformation of working-class areas by incoming middle-class families); ethnicity; and the possibility that greater levels of 'economic and cultural dynamism' in London provided a disproportionate stimulus to aspiration and, hence, learning and achievement. They concluded that gentrification was now no faster in London than elsewhere, that poverty was a greater driver than wealth and that white students had narrowed the gap between their achievement and that of high-scoring minorities. Finally, they did not consider the London factor to be 'convincing' (*ibid*: 54) or sufficiently different from a generation ago.

I am not in a position to theorize and neither can I demonstrate statistically which view is right. But the differences identified reminds us that non-school factors do have an impact on the inequities in attainment and other school outcomes explained in Chapter 1. Differences in the quality of schooling, at the most optimistic, can only make up to 22 per cent of the difference in outcome by the age of 16 (Rasbash *et al.*, 2010), as noted, with earlier authors putting this some percentage points lower (for instance Stoll and Fink, 1995).

There do have to be wider policies in place, though that is not the view necessarily of all the interviewees for this book, particularly those who began their careers in Teach First. But the Labour Government did put in place major social interventions that were seen to affect and relate to attainment, such as *Every Child Matters* (DfES, 2004a), and spelled out as such in the *Children's Plan* (DCSF, 2007) (see also Riddell, 2010). Much wider developments were implemented early on in the Labour Government – the New Deal for Communities and the Neighbourhood Renewal Strategy – following work by the Social Exclusion Unit (2001), then housed in the Cabinet Office but which no longer exists, just like its strategies.

Chapter 4

The emerging English polity for schools: Changing conceptions, identities and loyalties

The relationship that ... all the schools in [the County] have had with [the authority] has been through the ... [County] Association of Secondary Heads [and has] been challenged and ... diminishing over a period of years. [The County's] capacity to deliver school improvement work at a secondary level has been declining for a number of years ... and now has essentially disappeared ... there are no good secondary improvement staff really ... [Before] they were a mixed bag, of course they were but ...

(Thomas, secondary academy headteacher, shire county)

[There are] strange anomalies, and I think that's ... as much to do with the isolation of headteachers and the lack of, if you like, challenging debate in some authorities ... I think increasingly Local Authorities are pretty irrelevant in terms of the secondary sector ... Obviously you have the residual functions of things like SEN, but they're more to do with administering budgets in fair and transparent ways, rather than having any influence on the nature of teaching and learning, on school improvement kind of issues. So you could say the relationship has shifted to be more transactional around the residual statutory services of the local authority.

(Julian, education consultant)

The coalition government's white paper The Importance of Teaching strikes a startling new note. The improvement of schools, they are now told, rests primarily with them, not with government, local or central. The aim should be to create a self-improving system, built on the premise that teachers learn best from each other and should be in more control of their professional and institutional development than they have been in recent years.

(Hargreaves, 2011: 5)

Features of the emerging polity

The policy of moving towards a self-improving school system in England did not arise spontaneously after the Coalition Government was elected in 2010. Rather, its key facets were fundamentally rooted in the reforms of the previous 15 years at least. These include a move away from centralized prescription, on the one hand, and locally employed but nationally driven field staff, on the other, as Hargreaves (2010) put it. All staff employed locally to further the English education reforms described in Chapter 3 could be included in such a category. But many field staff were also employed centrally: at one meeting for managers and chief executives of private sector education consultancies alone, hosted at the Department for Children, Families and Schools just before the 2010 election, sixty pages of names were reviewed in the light of impending and anticipated budget cuts, according to a confidential source.

The move away from central prescription could be seen to have been informed by Barber's notion of a cycle from uninformed prescription, through informed prescription to finally informed (independent) professional judgement (Barber, 2004; Hopkins, 2007; Whitty, 2008). The second McKinsey school systems report (2010) had observed this apparent move away from central prescription in the schools systems they examined that were progressing from judgement categories of poor to fair, great and then excellent. According to McKinsey, this shift is therefore associated with increasing system performance.

At the same time, the budget cuts impending in 2010 became real enough after the election and, according to those I interviewed, became variably the precursor, pretext or rationale for strategic reviews of functions, nationally and locally, as a result of which some services were stopped. This represents an accelerated progression from what Lodge and Hood (2012) – as part of their characterization of the possible responses of the state to the challenges it faces – refer to as 'directing' behaviour on the part of the state to (perhaps barely) 'coping'. It had considerable consequences for the positioning of headteachers, as Arthur, quoted in Chapter 2, observes.

The argument for moving away from prescription while retaining some command-and-control elements has also been made in terms of the need to find alternative ways to raise outcomes. David Hopkins's 2007 book *Every School a Great School* is significant in this regard, not least because he succeeded Michael Barber as the chief educational adviser to the Secretary of State. The book is not only a commentary on the arrangements being put into place by *Higher Standards for All; Better Schools for All* (DfES, 2005), the third Labour White Paper, but it also points out that centralized prescription had achieved its limits in English schools as improvements in literacy and numeracy in particular had flatlined, and the first national targets, for 2002, had not been achieved. Something different was needed.

The new arrangements therefore increasingly involved seeking the expertise and capacity for continuing reform and school improvement within local school structures – no longer in LAs, and decreasingly in central government. The function of both the latter was developing towards the brokerage of support packages, especially after an unfavourable Ofsted judgement as described in the fourth Labour white paper *Twenty-First Century Schools* (DCSF, 2009a). These packages could be either from other schools or from the growing private and not-for-profit sectors increasingly contracted on a day-by-day, casualized basis. The developing national and local 'system' infrastructure and its designated system leaders were therefore slowly becoming the *only* means of change, underpinned *de facto* by the continuing budget cuts, especially in LAs, and the various theoretical justifications I explore next. A new system was emerging from the old.

Arguably, therefore, features of the school-led improvement system were beginning to be in place by 2010, as Hargreaves (2012b) and even Hopkins (2007) said. The process of change was accelerated by the rapid acquisition of academy status. James, the head of an academy chain when interviewed in 2013, described this scenario as 'practically complete' in the secondary sector. Although James might be right strategically, during the academic year 2014–15 some 60 per cent of state-funded secondary schools were academies or free schools – this is 1,997 out of 3,329 schools in England. For primary schools the percentage was just under 14 per cent (NFER, 2015). A further 1,042, however, were moving that way.

The apparent slowing of conversions pre-election variously reported by Mansell (2014b) and others, will no doubt re-accelerate with the election of a Conservative Government. With just one exception, *all* the headteachers of (still) maintained schools interviewed for this book had been examining academy status, they reported, in fairly pragmatic ways. They were 'biding their time', Martin, a secondary headteacher told me, until the outcome of the election was known.

The strategic point is that academy status took schools not out of LA 'control' particularly, but rather out of their professional, discursive orbit. This variably included their cyclical meetings with LAs, which had been diminishing, retreating or vaporizing anyway, as Thomas reflects at the beginning of the chapter. At the same time, academy status has affected the budget settlement central government makes to LAs, as it no longer deemed it necessary for them to provide any oversight or services to these schools (see DfE, 2014b).

Further, the promotion of free schools was clearly important to the Coalition Government politically – they have been repeatedly described as a 'flagship' policy in DfE literature, most recently in 2014 briefing documents I have seen for external members (non-civil servants) of the panel that makes recommendations on new applications to the minister. And these schools were new in the sense that individuals and groups of individuals (charities, universities, independent schools, community and faith groups, teachers, parents and businesses, according to the free school pages on the DfE website), often outside the mainstream education service, could bid to open a school that was not a conversion, intervention or fresh start. They are free in the sense that they, like academies, control the length of the school day and term, set their own pay and conditions for staff and do not have to provide the national curriculum. Legally, they are the same.

The Government provided funding to an arm's-length body, the New Schools Network (NSN), to promote and support new applications for free school status and then provide support for the schools once open. These new schools appear diverse in their origins and nature: one that I visited in an extremely deprived district in West London is an all-through 3–18 age-range school committed to ensuring all its students can attend a Russell Group university (Oxbridge and twenty or so other prestigious institutions in the UK). A free school in Slough was promoted by SASH, the town's secondary headteacher association. It was clearly still more effective than that in the shire county that Thomas works in. The Slough association, I was told, considered that the LA had not been acting swiftly enough to increase the number of secondary school places to meet rapidly increasing demand. The East Birmingham Network is another free school that makes alternative provision for young people excluded from school, managed by the secondary headteachers. Finally, I have come across a number of proposed and open primary free schools put forward by academy chains. They say their secondary academies could promote greater curriculum and pedagogical continuity and higher standards before secondary transfer, as well as providing new primary places.

Free schools are diverse and small in number – about 350 open by the time of the 2015 general election, compared to much larger numbers of academies. So although they represent some interesting and new additions to the polity, they do not yet represent an overall strategic change – or threat. The overall percentage is about 2 per cent of schools, including some other new forms of schools, such as University Technical Schools and Studio Schools.

The final feature of the developing polity is what an experienced Ofsted inspector described as the 'ratcheting up of expectations on schools'. I have noted the increasing floor targets year-by-year for primary and secondary schools that began in 2002 and are carrying on into the current government. Just as significant has been the replacement in 2012 of the old

Ofsted category of 'Satisfactory' (Ofsted, 2012) by 'Requires Improvement' (RI). Positively, this fosters the development of a national ambition for every school to be good or outstanding. Discussion about this change had begun under the Labour Government, but the obverse of the new positive aspiration for good or outstanding – more schools facing intervention – has not been universally welcomed by heads or teachers, according to LA officers and inspectors I interviewed.

The expectation of what *constitutes* good or outstanding has also been changing, as reflected in the downward modification in some schools' Ofsted status. The new Ofsted framework for inspection places greater emphasis on, for example, the 'impact of leaders' work in developing and sustaining an ambitious culture and vision in the school', and greater weight is given to 'the progress of pupils currently in the school rather than attainment and nationally published data' (Ofsted, 2015b: 6).

An Ofsted RI judgement has, since 2012, become the trigger for an improvement plan, to date put into place by the LA for maintained schools, and by the new Regional Schools Commissioners (RSCs) for academies and free schools since 2014. The RSCs meet regularly with their Ofsted counterparts and are central to the developing regionalization of the education state. All plans involve a brokered package of support and challenge. In a school where the leadership too requires improvement, Ofsted will revisit; and all the schools will attend the regular 'Getting to Good' seminars organized by Her Majesty's Inspectors (HMI).

At the same time, the concern of Ofsted with disadvantaged children (Ofsted, 2013; 2014b), led by a Chief Inspector with a strong 'moral purpose' according to one interviewee, no longer remains at the level of weighty comment. In one region of England, Ofsted had written to all schools where there were more than 20 percentage points' difference in attainment between advantaged and disadvantaged students (on the Ever6FSM measure), asking how they were addressing the gap. In the light of the differences in outcomes and in what children bring into school, the expectation that senior staff notice what is going on in their schools has to be welcomed. This represents a conscious shift into school improvement work by Ofsted, and seems to be part of a wider narrative about greater 'ambition' for children that may be developing. This too is to be welcomed, considering the overall inequity of student outcomes in England.

The professional preparation and continued training of teachers within a self-improving schools system must also be a significant, if not defining, feature of the polity. Some of the controversies about developments in this area need to be resolved eventually by evidence, but it is worth noting that the review of initial teacher training commissioned by the former Secretary of State (Carter, 2015) emphasized the importance of *appropriate* partnerships between schools and universities for teacher preparation. Rather than identifying a preferred partnership model, Carter says their nature should be determined and decided on by schools in a school-led system. In practice, this would mean the professional preparation infrastructure would be led from Teaching Schools and their wider Alliances. There is some evidence that this is the case in parts of the country.

Teach First sits a little outside this review as it is a charity and all its graduates study for a PGCE, albeit via an employment-based route (EBITT). It will remain, however, a strategically important and expanded route to acquiring qualified teacher status (DfE, 2010a). It appears to confer some advantage on its partner schools (Muijs *et al.*, 2012) as well as bringing new entrants into teaching (Hutchings *et al.*, 2012; Baars *et al.*, 2014) who have a commitment to addressing social injustice and a belief 'that a child's background should not limit the opportunities they have in education or life', as the Teach First website says. The 'impatient optimists' I encountered do talk about the need for more teachers to be ambitious for all children:

> I'm finding it very hard to find primary teachers who are not Teach First who are ambitious, like who want to be in charge, who want to make changes, who feel empowered, who feel energized ...
>
> (Edwin, principal, free school, originally a Teach First trainee)

This represents a changing expectation of, and in, the system assemblages, if not yet constituting an 'epidemic' (Hargreaves, 2003). Edwin, speaking about educational change in England, and considering the disadvantaged nature of the community his school serves, said that, by contrast, one of the interesting aspects of the:

> ... reform movement in the States, is that there's ... no sense of hypocrisy around the idea that these children need something different from what my children need. So you have a lot of people working in ... educational reform in America, which is a very much more radicalized, radical kind of space [than in England].

It is not possible to say yet quite what this space represents, how much of it there might be or what the systemic influence of free schools might be as they differ so much from each other, or to determine the wider significance of Teach First graduates. But the clear message of this Principal is echoed elsewhere. In its submission to the *Carter Review of Initial Teacher Training*

(2015), for example, The Association of School and College Leaders (ASCL) said that initial teacher education should:

> ... actively encourage teachers to see themselves as contributing collectively to social change, the common good and the creation of a fair society. We would like to see a renewed focus on the moral imperative of teaching and the purpose of education, which we believe will create a strong sense of energy, collective purpose and professionalism.
>
> (Carter, 2015: 25)

(Not) articulating the features of a self-improving system

Much consideration of national policy is an examination of intentionality, and at a naïve level it often stops there, not taking into account the complexity of realization. In this sense, the national prescription and target-setting – in a narrow range of areas – in the early phase of school improvement reforms could have been expected to have unforeseen consequences, and might thus have changed the relative priorities of schools and teachers. They did (Earl *et al.*, 2003; Riddell, 2013). And interestingly, Barber's most recent, very personal book (2015), advocating his deliverology method for, literally, running a government, devotes a whole section to unintended consequences.

The policy of the Coalition Government, however, was not quite like that. It made its intentions in certain areas clear in *The Importance of Teaching* (DfE, 2010a): it would act on the quality of entrants to teaching and the behaviour of children (together with the sanctions teachers could use), develop Teaching Schools, bring about greater school autonomy, set up free schools, 'dramatically expand the Academies Programme' (*ibid*: 12) and more generally 'put in place the structures and processes which will challenge and support schools to improve' and intervene in failing schools 'strongly' (*ibid*: 13). The White Paper said that in pursuit of its aim to see 'the school system ... become more effectively improving', it wished to see '[school] leaders ... leading improvement work across the system' (*ibid.*)', with the numbers of national and local leaders being expanded. At the same time, the Coalition's policy realization model, as in other areas (Riddell, 2013), included better data by families of schools and the development and advertisement of good practice through the Education Endowment Fund, which had been set up by two charities and was in receipt of public funding.

So the intentions of the freshly conceived system were apparent. Some elements were clearly set out, drawing partly from the London Challenge, as Greany points out (2014: 24). For him, what the White Paper had added up to was a 'hint' (*ibid*: 3) of what a self-improving school system might be. Drawing on other sources and his own research, Greany attempts to adumbrate the current policy formation against what he identifies as conflicting policy discourses – another shifting assemblage. Hargreaves comments on the 'startling note' of the White Paper (Hargreaves, 2014: 4) and the 'Government's offer to the profession to lead the *construction* of a self-improving school system' (my emphasis). This accords with my findings from the interviews of a system-in-development, still an emerging polity. Robert Hill (2011: 5) writes similarly about the 'proposals' in the White Paper that will 'promote school-to-school support'; he accords *The Importance of Teaching* the status of 'White Paper Strategy' (*ibid*: 5).

What these three commentators have in common is the National College for School Leadership, as it was originally named when set up at the University of Nottingham (David Hopkins's original home). Greany had worked there, as had Hill, and Hargreaves's work was commissioned from there. Originally tasked with providing programmes for the preparation, induction and development of school leaders, then extended briefly to LA Directors of Children's Services, the College was taken into the DfE under the Coalition Government and renamed the National College for Teaching and Leadership (NCTL). It took on the responsibility for the oversight of initial teacher training from the former Teaching Agency, which had also had several incarnations since the early 1990s.

The NCTL is significant and always has been. It has overseen fundamental developments in what can be recognized as significant strategic features of the developing polity, particularly of late. These include the previously compulsory National Professional Qualification for Headteachers, and then the professional development opportunities for serving and experienced heads. Thus all heads would experience its approach to leading for change. As reform evolved and its shape shifted in the 2000s, the NCTL took up responsibility for accrediting the new system leaders (at that time NLEs, LLEs and, since 2010, Specialist Leaders of Education or SLEs), who constituted the infrastructure for making a school-led system work. The NCTL now also manages the application process for Teaching Schools on behalf of the DfE. The aim is to have 600 of these by 2016.

Documentation on how to apply to become a school leader is available on the DfE website. The criteria are outlined for becoming an NLE, decided through three annual competitions. Heads need to be judged as outstanding and be responsible for at least one school that would qualify as such, not be below floor standards and be high-performing and improving over three years. These criteria also qualify the school as a National Support

School (NSS). To be a LLE, the head needs to be responsible for a good school, again determined by Ofsted criteria, and have senior staff with the capacity to work with other schools. Finally, the status of SLE, the newer aspect of the polity, is available to leaders at middle and senior levels who are used to support work and who understand and can communicate what 'Outstanding' means in their field of work. Potential Teaching Schools must also have an outstanding Ofsted rating, have experience of successful partnerships and an outstanding headteacher. Overall, then, the NCTL works closely and in tandem with Ofsted and the DfE; this can be seen as the triad of the education state.

Much earlier – from 2002 – the NCSL had managed and run another project that was highly significant for the present: the Networked Learning Communities Programme (NCSL, 2002; 2003). As the name implies, this was a project that joined and developed different school communities, not necessarily in the same geographical location, to share experience and develop new learning and knowledge collectively, through collaborative enquiry across their network. The contention was that the development of a professional learning community in a school was no longer sufficient on its own.

The National College, then and now, is a key mechanism for the implementation of Government policy, if not always directed as such, and became increasingly so when the move towards a school-led system became the intention. It develops this school-led narrative and supports it, codifying lessons from research. It commissions much of the research itself or draws on that which develops from projects (see, for example, Rea *et al.*, 2013; Stoll, 2015). The NCTL writes the system specifications for what are politician-originated and official-authored policy aspirations. It provides the iterative dialogue between policy detail and realization, which is 95 per cent of the task according to Barber (2015) and noted by Fullan (2001).

The four thoughtful and often profound think-pieces written for the NCSL by David Hargreaves (2010; 2011; 2012a; and 2012b) therefore merit consideration. Their status is interesting: in addition to much research citation (for example, Greany, 2014; 2015), they could be considered *policy interpretation* documents and at the same time *practical realization templates* and evaluation guides. Julian has used Hargreaves's documentation when working with groups of headteachers in a northern city, particularly the *Towards Maturity* paper (2012b):

> [I say to the heads] so let's have a look at where you are as a group
> ... Most of them are at what [Hargreaves] calls the beginning

stage of partnership competence ... [The heads] certainly don't know what the quality of teaching is [in one another's schools] teacher by teacher. So they are in groups who are technically there to support each other but they don't necessarily know who is the one who needs support in what. And they haven't got to the point where they trust each other [sufficiently] ... to share that knowledge between them.

(Julian, education consultant, speaking in 2013)

Julian went on to explain that, for primary headteachers, these groups were usually within one LA, often with their partner secondary school, although I have come across groups of primary schools working across such boundaries and not only in urban areas. But for secondary schools, Julian's experience was that the headteachers would generally look outside the LA boundaries for support, because they felt their 'relationships were less compromised than with their competitors within'. Another finding is that these relationships, or networks, were much more diffuse (or rich) at secondary than primary level, according to the headteachers. This was partly because of the competitive element.

So Hargreaves's 'maturity model' (2012: 7), with its three dimensions, 12 strands and trajectory grid (*ibid*: 5) *can* be used as a self-evaluation template by developing partnerships. Indeed it has been used in various NCTL projects, for example, by Teaching School Alliances (Stoll, 2015). But the model demands much of headteachers. Hargreaves said earlier (2010) that the benefits – he called them 'virtues' – of collaboration require the heads to 'co-construct' what their partnership is for, its priorities and how they will be implemented. To attain the required 'deep' nature (2012b), the partnerships or families need to develop the dimensions of 'trust and reciprocity', key components of social capital and a collective moral purpose far beyond what a teacher might feel towards his or her own students, to the point where they have the same commitment to achieving ambitious outcomes for students across all the schools in the partnership. According to Hargreaves, the partnership must develop strategies for evaluation and *challenge*, rooted in such trust, social capital and joint moral purpose. This may be the most difficult outcome to achieve to avoid defensive reactions.

But these partnership competences are there to underpin Hargreaves' greatest insight into how to transmit knowledge so that practice does change: *joint practice development*. This is enabled through the knowledge networks developed between schools about who is doing what, where and with whom, by building the trust and *earning* the right to challenge on the back of it – even to question what seems to be working well. There needs to be collective self-evaluation increasingly based on data.

The knowledge content of the four think-pieces by Hargreaves was not entirely new; he had begun to expound the possibilities of spreading knowledge through networks in his *Education Epidemic* pamphlet for Demos in 2003, drawing on a range of research and ideas, perhaps most intriguingly Raymond's notions of the 'cathedral' and the 'bazaar' (2001), based on examinations of open source software and the requirements for successful innovation. Famously, Hargreaves built his ideas on the notion of 'six degrees of separation' for all human beings (2003: 58). On this model the network begins to replace the hierarchy.

In educational terms, cathedrals of knowledge such as the literacy and other strategies may bring about significant change in classrooms, as Earl *et al.* (2003) found. But there are limits to what they can achieve when not all the teachers understand the pedagogical principles underlying the prescription: their learning may not have reached Fullan's third level of change (2001). This means they cannot easily adapt what is given to the needs, understanding and ambitions their pupils may present at any one time (Riddell, 2003). Also, they may not feel they can give themselves permission to do so. More of a 'bazaar' approach is required, according to Hargreaves, where teachers work together in the trusted networks to develop knowledge and their practice together or jointly.

Hargreaves contends that knowledge will be better generated in this way. He considers joint practice development in all the think-pieces. It involves, say, two teacher peers – or middle or senior managers – working together. The first may observe the second in their place of work, undertaking a particular activity or practice that they have developed over time and whose effects they have evaluated within their school. The two then return to the first school and examine how this practice can be implemented by the first teacher in the different context, through a process of mentoring and coaching with the second. The practice is often modified in the different school context through this process, enabling the second teacher in turn to deepen their understanding. Sometimes this process involves three teachers (known as a triad).

A new model of professional learning based on trust would arguably be preferable after the previous context of prescription, and this was certainly seen by teachers as one advantage of the London Challenge, particularly in the Keys to Success schools (Hutchings *et al.*, 2012). At the same time, Hargreaves's model presents the possibility of *outgrowing the limits* of earlier strategies, and of developing knowledge and ambitions against the concerns about the flatlining of attainment outcomes (Hopkins, 2007). In this sense, the model could be powerful. But although Hargreaves found in his school visits that the 'rate of progress [in partnership working] has been exceptional' (2012: 4), this did represent the ideal and, as he said in his first think-piece (2010), the self-improving system needs to be constructed. The question is by what process this can come about, and balanced against that are the roles of rising expectations and the regional state. From the evidence, this is, at best, mid-stream.

Hill outlined the key elements of what he called the white paper strategy (2011: 5) in moving towards this model. He was commenting on research undertaken into the perceptions and enthusiasms of existing school leaders towards the developing infrastructure of accredited national and local leaders of education. This NCSL piece was exposition, interpretation and implementation: Hargreaves (2010; 2012) was talking about the mature model, which needed and needs yet to be built.

However, Earley *et al.* (2012) had made what became much-quoted comments about how leaders fitted into one of four 'latent classes' in terms of their attitudes to policy and increasing school autonomy. These ranged from 'sceptical and demotivated', to 'apprehensive and hesitant to engage', to 'cautious while being mildly positive', culminating in 22 per cent of headteachers at that time who were 'positive and already pursuing new opportunities' (*ibid*: Chapter 5, no page numbers). Coldron *et al.* (2014) also developed the notion of 'well-positioned' heads, of schools that have achieved good Ofsted and data outcomes and who would fit into the last category. These terms offer interesting comparisons for headteacher interviews.

Greany's recent 'review of evidence and thinking' for ASCL also reports that the system leadership capacity – the infrastructure of the self-improving system (my words) – remains 'patchy' (Greany, 2015: 4) in providing school-to-school support. He finds that, because of the decline in local LA infrastructures, the flow of rigorous evidence about practice as described earlier is haphazard. He expresses the dilemma especially clearly: the question in such a school-led system must be how to 'incentivize leaders to shape their own local solutions without compromising equity' (*ibid*: 5). This issue is at the heart of the present book. ASCL had issued a 'blueprint' for the future 'authentically school-led system' (Cruddas, 2014: 15) that Greany's review was intended to inform. The blueprint is rendered slightly outdated by the 2015 election result, but senior staff in schools could be expected to welcome such a shift in the light of the governance issues considered here, and the reconfiguring of old power structures that is taking place.

The shifting landscape of schools and the evolving state: Forcing the pace?

As Woods and Simkins assert, the Coalition Government, through the Academy Act 2010 passed weeks after it assumed power, instigated the most 'radical *systemic* change since the mid-1980s' (Woods and Simkins, 2014: 324) in the structure of English schools. According to Bangs *et al.* (2012: 187) the change was 'seismic'. The Government forced the pace of change, eliminating the need for academy conversion to be an intervention in response to poor attainment or Ofsted inspection as before. And it began the process before the election. One of the headteachers interviewed explained:

> We were a converter … we were invited by the Government before they even got into power. Michael Gove contacted us … we went to Westminster and [at a large meeting] he said he would like us to be one of the earliest converters. However, the LA held us back a bit in our conversion process and we didn't convert as quickly as we would have wanted. However, we were one of the first.
>
> (Peter, headteacher, secondary academy)

This extract from a well-positioned headteacher whom I interviewed highlights some of the themes in conversion. As he says here, a good many headteachers were invited to a meeting in London where they were addressed by both David Cameron and Michael Gove before the general election of 2010. Some schools then began the much-simplified process to become a converter academy (now to be made simpler still) – with no required methods of consultation or parental ballot – shortly after the election. Others took longer.

Academization involves a change of legal status, with implications for the transfer of staff and land (see the DfE website for the process) and a change of governance. It is a *conversion*, however, and some converter academies have retained many features from their earlier identity including their name and the members of their governing body, but not as nominees of the LA. For others becoming part of a multi-academy trust or a chain (about 24 per cent of secondary academies in 2015), the governance arrangements may well change if there is but one governing body or board of trustees for all the schools.

While academy status began as the preferred model of governance at the start of the Coalition, there then came recognition that it was 'not the only model that succeeds', with the change in Secretary of State in 2014 (Vaughan, 2014), and now it has again become the most favoured model (Conservative Party, 2015). After the 2015 General Election the new government announced yet further change: they will make it possible for the new RSCs to intervene in schools that are coasting even if they are LA-maintained. Here, intervene means convert.

But a change in governance, albeit not always dramatic, can only bring about a change in direction or attainment if it enables *something different* to happen or something to stop. For Her Majesty's Chief Inspector (Ofsted, 2015b), it may well be leadership that needs to be different, but good leadership does not develop automatically with a change of status. More important is the sort of improvement plan described by Donald at the top of Chapter 3. That certainly does depend on leadership – which changes in his chain – but implementing the plan successfully is what is also really needed. It cannot be said that there is an academy model for change *per se*, therefore, unless it becomes the *only* governance model by which change can be initiated in England. What is crucial is what happens next in the school, whoever or whatever initiates it. And plans do not always work.

Public discussion about conversions, for example in support of local campaigns, particularly against forced ones, has ranged over a number of issues, as reflected on the Anti Academies Alliance (AAA) website. The AAA is an umbrella organization that works with local groups to campaign against conversion and free schools. These issues include disputed evidence about attainment, arguments that no change in status was needed and the nature of democratic oversight of schools so local groups feel they have some say in their children's education.

Different matters are at stake here. Alan, a campaigner against academization, was of the opinion when I interviewed him in 2014 that under Michael Gove 'revolution before the election [was] clearly … his agenda'. For Alan, this revolution of converters and free schools was about 'leaving education open to allow smaller and larger businesses to take control of schools'. In his experience, however:

> … there are very few forced academies because in most cases what had happened is that the governors had been going along with it … They had volunteered … [But] a forced academy – that is a very different beast.

The 'revolution' could be said to occur in an LA area where there has been such a large number of academy conversions that the LA's central grant is changed significantly, allied with further enforced budget cuts. Schools consequently cease looking towards the LA for much – and certainly not for the perceived value of democratic oversight.

I sought to explore the notion of democratic oversight with Alan. We talked about the mechanics of electing parent governors, for example, but for him it was important that 'elected officials' had responsibility for schools. Most significantly, he said that:

> ... if you have a local authority, community governors ... you've got a better chance of considering all the issues within the school's community and therefore what running a school that meets all those needs, or meets the needs of children in that community [actually means].

This echoes the discussion about the imprint of the community on children as they enter the classroom (Kerr *et al.*, 2014). But this campaigner is not alone in identifying the effective oversight of state schooling as an important strategic issue. Having a funding agreement directly with the Secretary of State means being directly accountable to her, primarily via officials in the Education Funding Agency, the arm's-length executive agency of the DfE set up for this purpose in 2012. But there have been problems with the shift in responsibility towards that organization and the more general dispersal of power.

The NAO examined the work of the Agency a year after its creation (NAO, 2014). It noted the rapidly 'increasing rate and pace of growth in the demand for the Agency's services' (*ibid*: 5) because of the growing numbers of academies (and free schools), all needing timely allocations of funding. The NAO recommended changes to the Agency's incomplete data-collection, better risk management and better customer service. The House of Commons Committee of Public Accounts (2015) subsequently considered the oversight of schools *as a whole* by the DfE to be 'weak' in some regards, with some 'confusion about the roles of the Department, the [Education Funding] Agency, local authorities and academy sponsors' (*ibid*: 4), 'allowing schools to fall through gaps in the system' (*ibid.*).

Specifically, the Committee was concerned about school failure going unnoticed, making it more difficult to intervene in a timely way, although it acknowledged that the Agency had been developing its risk assessment model. In September 2013, however, the Committee noted that 179 open academies had met 'criteria for formal intervention' in terms of attainment outcomes or Ofsted judgements, but only 15 of these had received warning notices from the Department. There were similar – though numerically fewer – failings with respect to fraud, and the Committee, furthermore, did not consider that the DfE knew 'which formal interventions are most effective to tackle failure' (*ibid*: 5).

Any supervision system can have failings, of course, but both these reports highlight the problems of having different bodies involved in supervision that have incomplete understandings of their role. The increasing fragmentation of the system highlighted by Simkins (2015) and Greany (2015) must inevitably play its part.

It would appear from most recent developments that the articulations earlier in the Coalition of purer forms of adherence to market forces working by themselves, with schools being held to account by parent-consumers, have now been abandoned. The Governments before and after the 2015 Election have been moving to a more regional structure. In doing so, as Greany (2015) points out, the Government has also abandoned, or ignored, the possibility of developing the LA role further as a champions for parents and children (set out in DfE, 2010a and earlier Labour Government white papers in the 2000s), whereby LAs would scrutinize the quality of education of all education providers in their areas. This had been recommended by the RSA Academy Commission (2013) and had been hoped for by a number of the LA officers I interviewed. Arguably, it is also the direction in which Ofsted was pushing LA work (2013) with their themed inspections.

This highlighted regionalization was barely a year old as I prepared this book for publication. The RSC appointments were announced during the summer of 2014. Their responsibilities were those of the national Schools Commissioner so no new legislation was required. But the appointments were an obvious response to increasing academization, the complexity of oversight highlighted by the NAO and Public Accounts Committee and the need to develop further DfE capacity.

The new appointments were largely drawn from serving headteachers (five out of the eight, with one other an ex-head) and they were to be supported and advised by headteacher boards (HTBs) of outstanding academy headteachers. The boards have six members, four elected by fellow heads and the remaining two appointed by the responsible RSC. All these heads have release time of up to a day a week. So their job is also to act as system leaders, undertaking direct support work in schools where appropriate and agreed. In effect, this means that the regional state is headteacher-led and, again, there is no supervision by the 'elected officials' desired by Alan.

The powers and responsibilities of the RSCs were set out in a briefing paper for Lord Nash, a DfE Minister before and after the 2015 election, entitled *Future Academy System* and dated 19 March 2014. This paper was helpfully leaked to the *Observer* and *Guardian* newspapers and Warwick Mansell considered it in his regular Tuesday column (Mansell, 2014a). I have also seen a copy. Like their line manager, the Schools Commissioner, these new post-holders were to be the advocates for academies, as the Government's favoured form of governance, including for maintained schools that wished to convert.

But in addition the RSCs were tasked, as Mansell says, with building key relationships in their regions. The relationship with Ofsted has been mentioned, but also involved were those with academy sponsors, the churches, Teaching Schools and Alliances, and LAs. So these are crucial coordinating posts for, or even architects of, the developing infrastructure of the school-led system. At the same time, the RSCs will be supported by various teams, most of them not yet 'regionalized' (that is, relocated from London). This includes data and EFA teams, so they can also draw on additional resources.

However, the most significant aspects of the Lord Nash briefing document, I maintain, relate to interventions. Much of the leaked document consists of decision trees. From summer 2014, the RSCs were already set to be 'making decisions' on academy performance. The Minister first sets the framework for intervention on the basis of attainment outcomes or Ofsted judgements that fall below 'Good'. Recommendations for intervention in academies are then discussed and possibly agreed by the RSCs with their HTBs. The subsequent interventions, through brokered packages that draw on the local infrastructure, are then to be supervised and monitored. So the RSCs add a standards dimension to academy and free schools supervision, on top of the EFA's financial ones.

But this is where a strategic shift was signalled. As one of the RSCs said before taking up his appointment, he would also take an interest in low-performing maintained schools. The mechanism would be that one of the 'school brokers' who are staff of the national Schools Commissioner would approach him. The remit for academies and free schools would 'cross over' into maintained schools when a school had been identified as 'underperforming'. It would then fall to him to think about 'solutions', possibly including finding a 'sponsor' for the school to become a new academy.

Later, this RSC said he expected to 'work with' LAs and would ask what thoughts they had been developing about schools identified in their areas as at risk. If the LA had a plan, it would be reviewed a few months later, to see what the 'indicators' were. He memorably said that there would now be no 'beating about the bush' or 'hanging about'. The expectation was that change would be 'rapid'.

The mechanism identified here is academy conversion as the basis for an intervention in the school, where the RSC exercises the formal power under current legislation on behalf of the minister. In one sense, this is a reversion to the policies of the early 2000s. Conversion is not a sudden overnight process, however, and neither is it guaranteed success: it depends, again, on what it can give rise to. Hutchings *et al.* (2012) noted that the schools forced to convert to academy status as part of the London Challenge made no faster progress than unconverted schools. But on this basis there is no doubt that LAs will face increased pressure under the new arrangements, irrespective of their capacity to broker support or whether they have noticed a problem at all. Further, one of the first acts of the new Government in 2015, as we saw, was to advertise new legislation allowing the RSCs to intervene in maintained schools. This would clearly deal with the 'no hanging about' issue for coasting schools or others. But it also means that academy conversion now becomes the one model by which intervention in a school is initiated.

As a footnote to this section, both the main parties standing in the 2015 election had advocated some form of regional organization of central government to oversee schools. Had there had been a Labour Government, LA powers to plan school places would also have been removed (Blunkett, 2014). So this is without doubt the direction of travel for England. The House of Commons Education Committee began taking evidence on the role of RSCs in the autumn of 2015.

Free schools

If the Conservative Government's ambition to open an additional 500 free schools by 2020 is realized, these could constitute nearly 4 per cent of state secondary *and* primary schools (21,500) in England, though the phase balance of proposals by area will clearly be important. This is more significant than the current numbers of around 350 of diverse age ranges, missions and locations. Arguably, these are too few to make a strategic difference to local schooling systems, but there may be exceptions.

The NAO (2013) and the Public Accounts Committee (House of Commons Committee of Public Accounts, 2013) also examined some of the problems with developing the early free schools. According to the NAO, the assessment process had become much more rigorous than at the beginning of the 2010–15 Government, and this was reflected by comments made by someone I interviewed in 2014 who was working with free schools and who had worked on applications previously. Mark felt that DfE officials had become more 'conservative' now (and by implication, less radical than when the first proposals were made).

The interview panel making recommendations to the minister on new free school proposals is expected to consider a wide range of capabilities, drawing on briefing documents I have seen. Potential new free school proposers are advised by the NSN, the charitable body funded to provide support for such applications, another new non-state actor. The NSN ensures proposers have access to educational, financial, project management, governance, ICT, buildings, legal and marketing expertise, as well as experience of business start-ups (as explained in a PowerPoint presentation produced for a regional briefing meeting).

The NAO report also draws attention to the underestimation of the expanding capital costs involved in setting up free schools (echoed by the Public Accounts Committee), particularly when considered alongside the low take-up of places in some areas. But the NAO acknowledged, against the background of some controversy, that 'most primary free schools are in areas that need extra school places' (NAO, 2013: 7). Although some free schools are developed in response to the need for extra places, however, including those opened by academy chains (whose proposals are more likely to be accepted by the DfE according to Mark), the free school mechanism clearly cannot be the only one available if national demand for places is to be responded to adequately and strategically.

The free school 'movement', if it can be described as such, has brought new people into state education. They may or may not provide better experiences for their children than others; Ofsted judgements tend to confirm they do, though very few yet have the intended full age range of children. The free school I visited was certainly impressive, though it could not be thought to be widely representative of anything except that it was run by an 'impatient optimist' with enthusiastic staff, many of whom had come through the Teach First route.

On the other hand, according to Mark, no free schools were 'set up [to be] very determinedly individualistic'. He noted there are 'lots of different ways in which free schools are … working with the local schools'. And he was clear that the 'overwhelming majority of free schools are following, in some sense or other, the national curriculum'. He also said that, with a few exceptions he could name, 'the overwhelming majority of teachers in the overwhelming majority of free schools are qualified'. This is difficult to verify, of course, but Mark pointed out that 'parents want to know that their teachers are well trained', particularly with the uncertainty of some local school choice markets.

So the interesting question is whether the presence of free schools can make any difference to their local school systems or ecosystems. Such claims have often been made over the past twenty years or so for various new types of school, such as 'beacon' schools by the DfEE (1997), although this is not one of the criteria used to agree the opening of a free school. Some of the reported interactions of free schools with their local counterparts are interesting in this regard, but because of the schools' diversity there can be no simple blueprint for such work. And unless they are part of an existing chain, no free school could yet be part of the sort of developed local school partnerships described earlier. But neither are many academies nor maintained schools.

Mark makes a wider, more ambitious and perhaps less tangible claim about the systemic influence of free schools:

> They are never going to be numerous enough to be a kind of actual reality ... in a large number of areas, and ... a catalyst for change ... What ... they could be quite effective in doing is being trailblazers for looking at how the system could develop ... looking at what's possible ... A number of free schools are really very ambitious in terms of what they want to achieve for their pupils [and] ... there is some evidence to show that some [of them] are being successful.

He continued:

> ... although they might not have a substantive impact, they will kind of ... shift the conversation that's had around schools.

A paper published by the Policy Exchange (Porter and Simons, 2015) claims that, among other things, free schools do make this systemic impact. Except for the first schools opened in 2010, the authors say in every year 'the opening of a Free School is associated with substantial gains in performance of the lower performing primary schools nearby' (*ibid*: 6). They claim this effect goes 'even wider', with a new secondary free school being 'associated with above national increases for all secondary schools, with below average results, in every year from 2011 to 2014' (*ibid*.). According to the authors, the effects seem to be magnified in high poverty areas.

The paper gives a statistical analysis of the closest schools and also considers possible qualitative explanations based mainly on extracts from self-reported impacts described by headteachers themselves (page 28 onwards). The impacts are largely rooted in classic market considerations, with neighbouring schools marketing more ferociously, changing their provision and expanding the nature of their local offer in response to what the free schools had been doing. Without further investigation, it is difficult to confirm or refute these conclusions and whether any impact is due to other local factors. 'Associated with' does not mean caused. Nor does it seem possible to draw on international evidence to help in this regard – there must be some very local factors because of the individual nature of free school proposals (the schools themselves not yet being systemic). And Wiborg (2010), writing about Swedish free schools, supposedly a model for the English policy, said they could only be understood within their specific cultural and historical contexts.

Chapter 5

Foretastes of a school-led system: The shifting assemblage of governance and practice

In some local authorities there is among many headteachers a search for some form of what I might call collective tribalism. The fact of tribalism is accepted, but there is also a yearning for something above the tribes, a deep desire for the tribes to come together with a sense of place, often a town or district in a large local authority, in order to connect with a range of local social and children's services. It remains to be seen what new structures will emerge in the light of weakening local authorities and the rise of tribalism.

(Hargreaves, 2012: 32–3)

We've got a number of people who work in more than one school in terms of their roles ... One of the unseen benefits of developing the shared leadership structures is you've got a group of people who've stepped up to roles across the [chain] and have to be given more time to do that. But we've then created a layer of backfill for their internal roles and that's created an amazing opportunity for the next layer of leaders to start to show themselves.

(Dominic, head of academy chain)

Introduction to the data

The next two chapters set out in greater detail some of the data gathered over the second and third series of interviews. All of the interviewees are living the 'seismic' policy changes described by Bangs *et al.* (2011). Evidence of the nature of these changes and how schools and LAs try to adapt and influence them continues to accumulate as I write.

I interviewed people whose own positions and outlook were changing while the polity was reconfiguring round them, often between interview and follow-up. Images emerge of a decentred assemblage, as yet unsteered, as Ball and Junemann describe it (2012). Despite the predominantly positive comments recorded in this chapter that presage a school-led system, the current period of change is producing enormous uncertainty and insecurity even for those who are well positioned. Michael's comments expressed something of the weight on his shoulders in 2014:

> We *are* thinking about academy status – yes – because we need to revisit key areas. Three years ago we did this, but things have moved on ... The Regional Schools Commissioners are [now] significant ... Lots of people have views about what we should be involved in ... [We are] aware that we have status with two Outstanding judgements, but ... [nothing] lasts forever.

But, like almost all I interviewed, he remained positive:

> This is a really fantastic opportunity to build a ... really tight group of educational establishments under the right leadership [in this town] – we have a history of working together.

Spotting and realizing the potential of new arrangements in the ashes of the old, cloaked in the old clothing and words, is essential for system leaders (Hopkins, 2007). How do they maintain their ambitions for children and their families and commitment to their staff? This chapter begins with a small sample of the comments made about this deep commitment, introduced or counterpointed where appropriate with the sorts of doubts and uncertainties at the enormity of the task expressed by Michael.

The rest of the chapter is devoted mainly to an exploration of school-to-school working and partnership – not the same thing – as seen by the heads and officers I interviewed. It is set out by phase, though the evidence does not always fall conveniently into such a bifurcation – as nothing ever does – and I conclude with a review of the pioneering work in one LA I visited. I cover work conducted in, and by, academy chains – possible future, diverse models – and touch for the first time on the work and influence of the LA.

The motivations and moral purpose of headteachers in the light of uncertainty

Reflecting on his predecessor's entries in the school log book in the mid-nineteenth century, Michael expressed his view that the job of the headteacher is 'just as lonely ... just the same as it has always been'. His distant predecessor had confided his worries about an impending HMI visit and the results of a violent incident in the community being carried over into school.

Dominic, head of an academy trust, spoke of all the headteachers in his area feeling 'very isolated', with no one 'want[ing] to go first' with respect to academy status, 'but very definitely no one wanting to be the last to make the decision'. And Peter, a well-positioned academy head elsewhere talked about 'headship [being] lonely, very lonely ... You need to [be able] to bounce ideas off people'.

But Cameron, an experienced inspector and ex-headteacher, said that the continuing motivation for headteachers 'comes down to passion, with heads doing their damnedest [with] commitment, tenacity ... all heads have always needed that ... asking what makes the difference, what is having the impact?' Martin, whose secondary school serves a deprived area in the Midlands, speaking in 2014 gave an example of such passion. It is about, he said:

> ... how you're dealing with kids in the future here ... if we don't get it right for these kids, some of them will ... well you can't repeat your education can you? ... From society's point of view, we should be investing in everything that we can do. And particularly some of the most hard-to-place and hard-to-reach kids from some of the hardest-to-reach families. If you want society to be better, these kids have got to be educated and have got to come out with the vision of what life could be like for themselves.

Martin's school had just achieved a 'Good' verdict after years of hard work and so he was beginning to be well positioned, feeling 'mildly positive yet cautious'. The extrinsic motivators such as Ofsted had put pressure on him but not diminished this inner commitment. He didn't want to spend his life in a PFI 'contract culture', as he put it, with people hiding behind the contract.

In a similar vein, Alison, an experienced headteacher of an outstanding maintained primary school, reflected on a recently held 'farewell lunch' to which the local group of heads in this small unitary authority had invited ex-colleagues:

> And it's interesting to talk to them, you know. What do they miss? Without exception, they always, always say the children and the teachers. And they don't miss anything else. Which actually is a bit sad, I think, because you know it is about the buzz and it is about the change, and as a headteacher, what you can do to develop and change and improve and expand, in all those different ways, not just for yourself, but for all your teachers ...

And about fifty miles away Arthur described his own drive, to endeavour:

> ... to be the best you can ... keeping other people's workloads down by noticing what are the key things that have the biggest

impact on achievement, not attainment ... It's about, for me, happy children, wanting to learn and being motivated, enjoying their lessons ... [School should be] a pleasant place to be ... where they are allowed to be creative ... and make the best of their skills.

After talking for over an hour about the difficulties and challenges of the current arrangements, Richard, the head of a maintained faith school, described headship as 'a wonderful job. I mean you are fired by a sense of moral purpose, there's no doubt about it'. By way of illustration, he spoke of a school he had partnered in an inner city area that was still requiring improvement, but with 'the most wonderful headteacher and staff who are just so committed to those youngsters ... And the sense of aspiration [even in] these times'.

Thomas, head of a secondary academy that was an NSS, while speaking about 'heads feeling quite exposed and vulnerable' at the moment, also talked about his partner primary heads 'all doing a very good job for a long time in their community'. The principal of an all-through free school talked about headship being 'kind of a mission ... and it's about effecting social change; it's like a social justice thing, very much. And so I think that ... gives us the will to challenge and cajole and encourage and improve.'

Similarly, Andrew, a Midlands-based primary academy head of a school serving a deprived area, spoke of his wish to be in the classroom:

Because that's what, of course, you know, twenty five years and ... the four years of ... training ... give you. You want to get your hands dirty and you want to work with kids because that gives you the impetus as far as the work you do ... We're all about kids, working for our kids in our local community, let's ... really get to the nub of what we do.

Although there are many more comments that echo such sentiments, I conclude this section with the words of a committed primary academy head with a recent RI Ofsted judgement – so not so well positioned but still actually pursuing new opportunities – who talked pragmatically about wider developments, posing the strategic dilemma for a school-led system:

We need a school system that meets the needs of children: what in the new landscape is the best thing for this school now? ... But it's dangerous if people are in power without moral purpose ... [and] how can [we] develop system capacity without losing the instructional focus at our own schools?

School-to-school relationships

The moral purpose and sense of mission among headteachers – and among LA officers, inspectors and private sector consultants – were not hard to find. One fundamental question for a school-led self-improving system is how school leaders can both sustain this moral purpose and transfer it to children in other schools. What mechanisms will enable and sustain them in this (Hargreaves, 2012b)? Headteachers of primary and secondary schools, of academies and maintained schools alike, described rich patterns of relationships with other schools, some sustainable and long-term (in partnership), others short-term and sometimes contractual or quasi-contractual (working together). Such relationships sustain them.

Inter-school relationships start for different reasons: some grow from the desire, expressed by all the heads I interviewed, to go on developing and improving. Sometimes this is voluntarily, but it can be a response to external pressure to improve, or a result of a full-blown intervention following status transformation. Discussions with heads about development and improvement often began with the school's relationship with the LA's School Improvement Adviser (SIA) or School Improvement Partner (SIP). Relationships with these staff appeared to be better when they had been sought out by the headteacher rather than appointed by the LA.

Secondary school partnering and development

Selina, the head of a girls' school in the Southeast, for example, described the first LA-appointed SIP they had as an:

> ... utter waste of time and money. When we became an academy, we used a headteacher ... who had just been made a Dame and who was brilliant. Each visit we went through what we were concerned about and she brought a fresh pair of eyes each day she was with us.

The school changed its SIP after a few years, however, because it needed to rediscover that 'fresh pair of eyes'. Uniquely, though, this school had deeper relationships with other girls' schools in the region, which were sufficiently distant not to pose any competitive threat. Staff visited the other schools to look at particular aspects of provision (for example, the best ways of meeting the cultural aspirations of the communities served), showing some signs of joint practice development in its early stages at least.

Sometimes local secondary heads' associations, not the trade union, offered a variety of services. In Selina's area, different schools offered a range of senior and middle management training sessions at low cost. The cost of subscriptions to the associations varied. As Selina remarked, now '[we are] friends with everybody': the school would offer days on particular topics, telling the partner schools 'we are doing X, just come.'

In contrast, Thomas spoke candidly about the decline in his local secondary heads' association (as quoted at the top of Chapter 3), with other heads of academies like him dropping out of meetings. He described his county as 'big and empty' geographically. Although the headteachers in his part of the county continued to meet on some matters, for example students at risk of exclusion, he never visited schools in other parts of the county though his school had 'very actively sought out other local schools … to do paired work'. The day after the interview he was visiting another secondary school not far away to 'do paired lesson observations for some middle leaders. And we've had leadership teams from each of these schools come and visit us to do observations'.

This NSS was delivering a range of work. It seconded a member of staff for a day a week to the leadership team of a neighbouring school after it received an inadequate verdict at the request of the LA. Thomas's heads of science and maths, he explained, were 'going over' to another school, in a different authority, that had had a similar verdict. The head of modern foreign languages and an advanced skills teacher in maths were working for parts of the week in a school in a different authority that had problems with attainment. Similarly, a deputy head had undertaken a four-day review for a college and the head of science had mentored a new head of science in another local school. Finally, the school was in discussions with the DfE and the newly appointed RSC about sponsoring an academy in another LA.

Thomas described how, for his own development, training as an Ofsted inspector (part of the NLE role), working with a 'group of heads of outstanding schools … felt like quite an investment this year' and said he was already 'bringing things back'. But he observed that 'one of the risks for the schools that are relatively successful is that it is very hard to find that very critical person doing the challenge'. He described 'several cycles of trying to find the right School Improvement Partner', and remarked that 'really you should be changing them [because] three or four years in … they become institutionalized … and the relationship between the head and them can become too cosy'. This school bought someone in to advise the governing body about pay progression.

By contrast, Dominic, reflecting on when he had been the headteacher of a secondary academy, had employed an SIA originally provided through the LA (first being bought in by the school and then by his academy chain – when it was set up) to conduct his performance management. This was arranged at 'a large meeting where we do the review', which included the chair and vice-chair of the board – the employer of all the staff in the chain's four schools – and the chairs and vice chairs of governors of the four schools. Sometimes the secondary academy bought in 'extra services' from this SIA, the retired headteacher of a high-performing faith school.

The chain was in the process of employing a retired primary headteacher and Ofsted inspector as an SIA for the two primary schools (Cameron). The arguments the headteacher gave for 'having one person who's looking across the piece is that actually they will be able to see where there's an issue in one school and know where the capacity is in another school'. An LA officer could have made a similar case for the role of the 'middle tier' in a previous era.

Dominic's chain came about after the lead school, where he was head, was approached by the LA to 'take over' a neighbouring secondary school that had been judged inadequate by Ofsted and whose headteacher had left. Recently it had been thinking more broadly about developing 'English, science and maths lead practitioner roles' for its primary and secondary schools. And the two secondary schools were now pairing members of the leadership teams to 'go and spend a day doing … a shared activity in the other schools so they get beneath the surface of what's going on, so we do get that sharing of best practice both ways.' Whatever the outcomes of this work, it was part of an attempt to 'equalize the roles between the two schools' to overcome a perception of takeover. It has the shape of joint practice development, as described by Hargreaves.

Other secondary schools I visited had been on the receiving end of quasi-enforced collaboration, including through the National Challenge when their outcomes were below floor targets. Martin, a maintained secondary school head, said that because their 'results were [so] shocking, [there] had been discussions with the LA … and … with the head of a fairly local school with lots of ambition who actually phoned the governors and said "I will take over the running of the school and sort it all out"'.

This took place within the context of fierce local competition 'from immediate neighbours' in the metropolitan area, with schools 'marketing quite aggressively, on the back of football tickets and on buses' and offering free uniforms. Martin is the head quoted earlier who felt that the school's future was 'in our hands now', and who was 'in control of those interventions'. The first intervention had involved an imposed task group 'to hold us to account', chaired by an HMI. The task group pursued what the head described as a forensic focus on the progress children were making and how it was affected by teaching deemed 'inadequate'. Now 'everyone was on top of any form of under-achievement'.

The school has its 'own version' of the task group which is a 'development opportunity, so that the subject leaders know what is expected of them in terms of raising standards and raising attainment', rather than being subject to external accountability. The 'job descriptions for subject leaders and seconds in department' had been 'rewritten totally [so that] they understand really exactly what their role is in terms of raising standards'. They now work with a SIP who was also an HMI, and the regular sessions with him are attended not just by the 'senior staff [but] all subject leaders … at Key Stage 3 and 4'.

This maintained school was examining the possibilities of forging 'links … particularly with primary schools [through] a multi-academy trust'. Martin told the story of the progress made by the school he led and characterized it as one of external pressure and being held to account, against the background of neighbouring schools offering take-overs and of a senior LA officer also offering himself to the school's governors. But Hargreaves – surely correctly – argues that long-term established partnerships need to be based on trust, such as that spoken of by Selina, the head of the girls' school. This indicates that Martin's school's relationship needs yet to develop for it to be long-lasting, as in the academy chain where Donald was head.

The secondary headteachers I interviewed offered other observations on school-to-school relationships. Peter, head of one of the first academies to convert under the Coalition Government, outlined some of his work as an NLE. His school had been outstanding in Ofsted terms for ten years and served wards that were among the 10 per cent most deprived in the country. He described some of his visits to two neighbouring schools, one on a weekly basis, 'just for a chat with the head … no formal agreement', having what he termed a 'coaching role' with him. His being an NSS, Peter said other schools often approached it for help with particular aspects of development work, often quite informally at first.

Peter also talked about how the school's SIP – provided originally through the LA – had asked him to meet the governors of a school in another LA, who then asked him to 'cast an eye over the school'. He agreed to work with the school only on the condition that the headteacher – who was not 'on top of the data' and was not strategic, involving himself 'with everything, from the day-to-day to the mundane' – would be replaced. Accordingly, the governors offered his post on a temporary, then permanent, basis to the existing deputy head, a person considered by the NLE to have 'got the staff working with him'.

This is a powerful position to be in. Peter's school signed an agreement with the LA to work with the school. There was money for only the first year, but the engagement lasted another two. The developmental power of the relationship was that, as Peter made clear, it was not just a takeover by a better school. They did not tell schools they partnered what to do or to simply adopt practice they found in their school: the new partner was expected to develop its own. This was about working together; Peter's school would get just as much out of it: 'when we start supporting schools, our vision was not to take over. We want a non-threatening approach to school-to-school support' that is based on trust. 'We learn as much, of course, by supporting schools as they learn from us'.

Peter told the new acting head of the SIP-identified school that 'we knew what we did here [in our school]; some of it would work [in yours], some of it wouldn't... You can't copy it. You can take the best bits and see how it fits in with yours ... and that's what the collaboration is all about'. His view was that collaboration is all too often seen by the DfE as a takeover, but he preferred other models: for some schools, who were 'just on the verge of getting there, there are other solutions'.

This remark echoes that made by Thomas, similarly an NLE:

> There is always great practice in a school that is superficially failing. And there are areas that we need to sort out all the time here, so it's never a ... sort of binary good or bad school situation.

Richard, the head of an outstanding faith school elsewhere that served very mixed communities, made similar observations about the process he had been involved in with another school. He had been asked to step in by the LA after it decided not to close it as part of the LA's secondary review. This school, according to Richard, had a reputation (and a roll) that had been declining for twenty years, plus an accompanying and developing structural budget deficit. If unchecked, the school would have failed to meet floor targets.

He offered 'three years of leadership' to the school, with himself as executive headteacher, although again LA funding was only available for the first year. He described the arrangement as a 'collaboration' and said he had resisted pressure from the LA for a hard federation that would have involved just one governing body or set of trustees. There was, however, a formal memorandum of agreement between the governing bodies and the diocese. Describing the work he did, he told me, after 'years in headship, I don't regard it as some kind of secret recipe. There's a very short list of things to just keep getting right'.

Some of his work at the partner school involved taking opportunities that had been missed in the past – putting right the relationship with the governing body, involving staff, celebrating success (for example by beginning all staff gatherings with a 'what's going well' question), addressing the budget deficit by restructuring the staff and being straight while doing it. But new staff were appointed, including a new lead for teaching and learning which Richard considered the most important area for his own school. This new post-holder developed a school-wide approach to marking and performance management with the staff and an agreed policy and practice approach to teaching and learning. But all this was accompanied by an informal rather than structured programme of 'lots of days of colleagues visiting each other, which ... was kind of mutually nourishing'. Richard's school never gave the impression, he said, that his was the successful school helping out the less successful one. The leadership teams met with each other, had similar job titles and developed 'ideas from each other', such as on joint residential events. They also developed an off-site register to ensure that students were tracked when involved in activities or lessons in another establishment, as has become common post-14.

At the time of the interview, the three-year formal agreement was just finishing, though established professional contacts were expected to continue. Richard described his school as having 'a lot of internal capacity' despite all this work and had formed other links through heads of schools of similar faith and his neighbours. He is another formally well-positioned head, but he too outlined some of the uncertainties of his professional life, such as being excluded, he felt, from a local academy collaboration. He was concerned about the fierce competition between local secondary schools and the 'volatility of the Ofsted regime'.

Although made in different circumstances, these observations on school-to-school collaborations could be seen as the basis for the longer-term partnerships considered by Hargreaves. The arrangements described by Peter and Richard arose from a need to address school weaknesses, were intended to be seen as collaborative – unlike some of the offers made to Michael and his school – and both, interestingly, were led by heads with a simple list of matters to be attended to when schools needed new direction.

Peter had his own version of the five Keys to Success for his school (which I do not name, to preserve anonymity) that echoed the emphasis on 'getting the basics right' in the quote from Daniel at the beginning of Chapter 3. Some Ofsted inspectors interviewed also used this phrase. The intention was to establish trust between staff groups, but it is not possible from this evidence to decide whether this has been achieved.

More on academy chains

The school-to-school support described by all the heads of academy chains was integral to the nature of their work. The large national chain headed by James, with schools in both the private and public sectors, put great emphasis on bringing together young people from different social backgrounds through enrichment events, particularly as it acquired new academies serving 'challenging communities'. One of the private schools provided coaching for Oxbridge entrance. Even with separate governing bodies, all the staff in the academies were employed by the same charity so they could be moved around to different schools (another prerequisite for joint practice development). But given the geographical spread of the schools, James, the chief executive, made much of 'plus one' groups, whereby all staff in the chain took on one extra piece of work that contributed to the wider organization. There was a curriculum group, for example, and subject networks were in the process of being established to share good practice and ideas, and debate issues. NLEs are also involved where 'strong schools are sharing with other schools' to codify practice, as James put it, so that it can be used to review progress. Common ways of doing things across the chain were important, such as performance management and accountability. Interestingly, here too there was a short list of matters to attend to when an underperforming school was being added to the chain. Although the chain tried to 'have a fairly bespoke solution', James observed that:

> ... the ingredients of that are not any great secret ... the right governance, the right leadership ... in headship, the right senior team ... putting in some kind of sound tracking systems if they don't already exist, making sure you've got a fit-for-purpose staffing structure and restructuring if necessary ... [with] professional development for staff. And sticking to a pretty clear improvement plan, and so on.

He was slightly less hands-on than his two counterparts in the other chains I visited, a function of size and geographical spread, and they had no 'supply of interim leaders ... waiting to parachute into place'. But they did have an education advisory team that would be 'getting in there, getting alongside, providing support and direction'. This work was overseen by heads of primary and secondary education. James's chain also had what he described as 'a sort of associate status ... a loose affiliation' with a number of Teaching Schools in various parts of the country. If the chain was confident that these schools were aligned in terms of 'ethos and values' they were sometimes used as preferred partners.

Daniel, the chief executive of the third chain with a smaller group of schools, was far more directly engaged with all of them. He had appointed the heads of all the schools, except for two primary converter academies that 'chose to join us'. He described the 'considerable amount of time' he invested in this process, visiting applicants in their schools for half a day each. He told me:

> ... the school improvement journey fundamentally sits on the quality of the principal and the leadership team that they work with, and I have to be convinced that we have that quality at that level ... because you can't get that wrong.

This chain was originally based on one outstanding school and had taken on extra schools by agreement with two LAs, which had a 'fairly light touch' with respect to the improvement plans the chain had developed (which he liked). At the time of the interview (late 2013), the chain had just taken on two new schools, one of which had been in special measures. For this school, the chain had appointed an intervention team and another principal had taken on 'an executive role' to oversee the improvement. The vision was 'about getting back to good as soon as possible'. Daniel, too, described a model of:

> ... some very, very clear things that we need to do with our new schools to accelerate them to being secure in the first two years. The first year is usually quite ropey because, as you take the lid off a school, you realize the depth of the challenge. So year one is often not as rapid an improvement as the DfE would like, but year two is, when we've been able to sort some of that mess out and then move forward with it ... My experience is that if it's to see the kind of transformation [that is needed] ... then it's a two-to three-year project.

And as an interesting footnote, he added:

> I'm always suspicious when you see schools that have done it rapidly in year one, because that must be about quick fix, and I'm not interested in quick fix. I want us to be able to sustain an improvement over five years ... make people really clear what the expectations are and give them time to deliver.

Not surprisingly, he laid great store by personally doing the performance management of all the principals in the chain, even when they had achieved a good Ofsted judgement. But he recognized that this would be unrealistic as the chain expanded, particularly over a wider geographical area. He met the principals once a month, though they also needed to meet more frequently for 'line management purposes' with the two executive principals in the chain, one primary, one secondary. But his job was to question: 'how do I challenge them, how do I support them to become even better at [raising achievement]?' He would be 'focusing much more on the strategic plan and their development. I'm coaching them as leaders'. When it came to 'projections and results', he wanted 'to know the story behind them', but the details of developing the intervention would be left to the executive principals.

So this chain's approach, according to Daniel, was more towards the 'control' end of the spectrum than 'autonomy', as he himself said; the central team have a 'high level of presence in schools', meeting every Monday morning and Friday afternoon to 'review the week'. Their work involves undertaking 'no notice reviews', but this is partly, no doubt, because the chain has been involved in intervention: according to Daniel, the work has been largely about 'sorting out challenging schools' in its part of the country, where 70–75 per cent of the 'schools are in a position where they need quite a lot of care and attention'.

A different sort of professional trust may have developed here – confidence in the very strong leadership of the chain. It is arguable whether this yet entirely meets the criteria described by Hargreaves for mature partnerships, but it may well do for the first stage of a school-led system, which I argue in the last chapter, on the grounds of this interview data and the copious documentation available on the chain's website. The 'maturity' criteria might be realized when all the schools achieve the 'at least good' status and outcome data are improving.

For example, Daniel spoke of the importance of the agreement across the chain for making contributions to development work. 'The principals [see this] as part of ... their collective responsibility for all the kids'. This is *de facto* Hargreaves's collective moral purpose. At the same time, Daniel has been carefully developing a collective identity across the schools, by meeting all the staff together (over a thousand), twice a year. This, he told me, is the only time he is able to communicate priorities directly with them all. Six smaller annual meetings for staff across the chain are held on a subject basis. Collective solutions are being sought to common problems, for example effective targeting of pupil premium funding, including a central provision funded by a top slice, and in particular the infrastructure for development needed by all schools even when they have moved into the favoured upper reaches of the Ofsted judgement stream (mature partnership). At the same time, less formal contacts have developed through such initiatives as chain football and rugby teams. All the staff I spoke to informally as part of my visit were clearly very proud to work for the chain.

Building capacity for system-building

In Daniel's academy chain a team of over forty SLEs has been built up, all accredited by the National College. They were deployed on a monthly basis by the chain's Teaching School, as they are mostly employees of the chain, though a few worked in schools outside it. The chain's schools were expected to donate SLE time to working in other schools, and in return for this timetable commitment they received broadly equivalent development time towards their own improvement plan priorities.

Peter similarly outlined the work of the 17 SLEs within his academy's local Teaching School Alliance. Those on the staff of his school were given a morning or afternoon off timetable; he described his staffing situation as being seven over at that time. This allowed their deployment to other schools or, if they were not so deployed, their involvement in development work on site. This school had changed the timetable to create additional capacity on Wednesday afternoons, when the students had a variety of skills lessons taught for example by sports coaches, while others had catch-up lessons. Some afternoons were used to support other schools as part of the NSS work. For example, sixth form students had been bussed to other schools to work alongside students there. These Wednesday afternoons created capacity for all staff to have 'two hours of CPD [continuing professional development]' a week, at a time when they were likely to be receptive rather than at the end of a working day when they were tired.

Similarly, the girls' school referred to earlier, also an NSS, offered SLEs in data systems that involved a business manager. Two of the staff were ex-advanced skills teachers from an earlier scheme involving outreach from excellent teachers. The school also offered specialisms in Gifted and Talented provision and music. Its SLEs were offered 20 per cent non-contact time, or a day a week off timetable. As part of the NSS role, this had allowed them to offer support to schools in what the head called deprived areas in other parts of the country.

A crucial part of the capacity to be created for a school-led self-improving system must be developed in the leadership team, especially when an NLE or LLE is out of school working elsewhere. All the headteachers involved in this work, both primary and secondary, considered the acting-up experience given to staff covering for them to be vital in developing as future leaders. In Peter's academy, a rotating development post of associate head had been created in the leadership team. The post holder was based in the head's office, reassuring the members of the team that they would not come back from development activity in other schools to find problems on their own turf. All these schools were 'growing their own' future leaders.

The expectation of a self-improving system is that expertise will be sourced from *within* the network of schools to support improvement – and especially to help schools that require improvement. Therefore the development of the appropriate capacity is crucial, now that none exists elsewhere, least of all in LAs. To realize the model of continuing joint practice development, bearing in mind the reciprocity of the relationship, the staff who are supporting, coaching and mentoring colleagues need to be present in the classroom of the supported teacher even when trust has been established. And this needs to be paid for in one way or another by providing appropriate cover or timetable adjustments. Capacity is a key issue now and for the future.

Secondary summary

There is no space to detail all the rich partnership and innovative development work taking place even in this relatively small sample of secondary schools, as described by their headteachers and generally corroborated from their school or chain documents when available. Heads reported working in a variety of collaborative arrangements, some of which were clearly very fulfilling professionally, and rewarding for their own schools.

But outside the chains – and sometimes even inside – heads often felt they did not belong to a single, consistent and sustained group. The experience of primary heads is different, as I discuss in the next section. But the sorts of deep relationships in mature partnerships described by Hargreaves – that have to be a long-term goal – depend on staff who are all sufficiently at ease with one another to enable joint practice development of a non-hierarchical kind. According to Hargreaves, this *does* depend on there being one grouping that schools look to primarily for their long-term deep development, though obviously they can engage other individuals and groups for specific pieces of work. This is the difference between partnership and short-term working, but it has not yet emerged for all secondary schools.

Primary school partnering and belonging

Alison described the decline of a local teaching school that eventually lost its accreditation:

> [There was] absolute chaos and a real mess, and I think the problem with it was that it was far too woolly – it didn't go anywhere. It got itself into a big mess financially, big, big mess financially … It couldn't deliver, for all sorts of reasons, the head got very ill … it was in a downward spiral. A lot of the primary schools joined that, thinking that would be their answer – their saviour to everything.

There would no doubt be lessons to be learned from a detailed case study of this formerly successful school, but the comment illustrates the general uncertainty facing primary heads. It is apparent in earlier comments and in one made by Julian, the education consultant, that many headteachers feel they are 'Billy no-mates' (he is a Yorkshire man). It also shows potential vulnerabilities in a school-led system, a feature of a decentred shifting assemblage – no one was available to step in at that time or ensure the right thing happened. As a system leader, Alison had made various efforts to develop replacement provision, unusually involving regional associates of the National College.

Alison also spent some time describing the motivational aspects of her work with other schools as an NLE, echoing some of the secondary heads' experience. She had applied for and achieved the status following the work her staff had done in assessing other schools for a prestigious national award. The attendant NSS role brought many benefits to the school and the development of staff. At the time of the interview, Alison's school had just written a history scheme of work for the town within which her school is located, history being one of her passions. As an interesting illustration of the mechanism of the NSS role, no LA or anyone else had approached her immediately to support another school. After 'setting out her stall' on the National College website, she had asked herself the question: 'is it just going to happen? And it did happen, you know, surprisingly'. In other words, the role is sometimes mediated by a market mechanism.

Alison's school began its NSS work by supporting two schools in a neighbouring LA then one in her own. With help from the National College, this extended to a more distant shire county and joint CPD for groups of heads. From a development perspective, she had also paired up with a school in a different shire county, which was an academy (her school is not). This school had totally different conditions of service from those in Alison's school, and was more ICT-focused in its teaching compared to the fundamental orientation of arts in her own. This relationship was clearly very productive.

When we spoke, one of the school's assistant heads was acting head in an RI school; another was undertaking Ofsted training, and an aspiring deputy was a supernumerary deputy at another RI school. She described several support arrangements with other schools, and these kept cropping up during the course of the interview. Her SLE, assigned by her rather than the former teaching school, was a specialist in maths and science, 'a brilliant teacher [who had] amazing charisma … and wherever you send him … he'll work magic'. Alison described all her staff as having a 'niche and career path, so you're building that capacity all the time' through such development work. The NLE and NSS roles, as we have found, are intertwined.

She described her work in similar terms to that of secondary NLEs, and this appears to be the likely developing cross-phase model nationally. 'Belonging' does not fit with her work though. She had long associations with the town but this was only one town in her LA and the development work that was so enriching the progress of her staff had a wide geographical spread. She had also clearly played a major role in setting up an LA-wide partnership that had commenced with a recent meeting. These partnerships have a slightly different role from the sorts of deep partnering described by Hargreaves, and I will discuss them later.

But a large part of this data-rich interview was about the school-on-school support work, whose pragmatic nature appealed to me as an ex-LA officer. For example:

> … you go into a school and they're all very suspicious you know
> … But we found by working with learning support assistants, you
> [can] get them on-side. You train them up and then it filters up
> from the bottom, and that's always good … So some of my staff,
> teachers, would just go in for the first week and say, 'you know,
> here we are … we'll come and do some art with your children, or
> we'll come and do some music', and they like that because you're
> offering something that's non-threatening. So you've got a foot
> in the door, and you know that's how you move in. But that's,
> that's just us.

About another school her staff had been working with for some time, she said:

> The head's quite hard work ... I had to ... sort of work alongside their staff by back-door routes, but we've got to a stage now where their results have gone up finally. And that's because ... we've done a mixture of staff coaching and work with the children. So we've even brought their children here once a week [to work] alongside our Year 6 children; [we've done] lots and lots of sharing of moderated work, bringing their staff over here; making them feel very much that they're welcome. And, you know, [this] benefits us, which it does, hugely ... and also helping them out with issues that they then raised when they began to trust us ... So you get to that stage and then you can move on. So one of my staff in that school, for example, now, still goes in there every week just to teach SPAG [spelling, punctuation and grammar] and those results have gone up. But brilliant for that teacher too, because it was with a teacher who was a bit set in her ways, but a blinking good teacher, and you know once she's got the idea, and now knows that it's so well valued – a huge, huge beaming smile every time she comes in.

This is Alison's view as a well-positioned headteacher. It is similar to some of Daniel's comments, but raises again the matter of trust, achieved here partly through valuing the people with whom the school was working. But this also depends on who is available to do the work and how they can be relieved from teaching, in a way that is satisfactory for the children. For this head of a large primary school the capacity issue was primarily about adjustments to the timetable.

Generally there was external funding for some of this work, but not all. Arthur explained that when he took over his shire county primary school, then with a notice to improve, 'so many people came in and it was all paid for, not by us', but by the LA. His school, based on a more traditional model, had 'tended to use people who ... [were] still working for the LA', and still did so. His primary loyalty was local: he felt 'positively about what is provided locally and the idea of cluster schools working together'. He went on:

> It depends where you are and, you know, who's in your cluster, and how well you get on with people and all those personal things. But most good headteachers, I think, have positive

working relationships with other heads whom they know they share values with and swap ideas with, and trust.

He illustrated the constructive nature of such work with reference to the implementation that year of both the new national curriculum and reforms for children with special educational needs and disabilities (SEND):

> So when it's come to things like the new SEND reforms and the curriculum, my leader for maths, for example, has worked alongside the other leaders from each of the cluster schools, so that they together can address ... what we need to do to make sure we're fully aware of the changes for the new national curriculum. And they've done it together, and ... rather than my SENCO struggling to do [the SEND offer] on her own, we've got the SENCOs from the cluster together and so they're going to write a school offer which is going to be pretty much the same for every school in the cluster.

This school had achieved a 'Good' Ofsted judgement, although its vulnerabilities in this regard and the implications for confident long-term development will be reflected on later. Arthur felt it was 'a bit of a cuspy school at that time'. The significance here is that the local cluster in a very rural area had been taking the initiative by itself, based on its past history. No one else could, physically, achieve this on a routine basis, even an NSS.

That this happens is essential for a school-led system. Nevertheless, Arthur also described some of the shifting loyalties in his area precipitated by the possibilities of academy status. He is quoted earlier in the book. Since two primary schools had joined local secondary school-led chains, for example:

> You can just sense the tension, the competition there, which is the opposite of my idea of being mutually supportive ... It was very much us and them ... be careful what you say. My previous experience of any group of headteachers was just share, share, share.

So this was increasingly affecting mutual loyalty. And in this rural area, attendance at meetings and involvement could vary too. Arthur told of how this varying level of involvement affected relationships, such as in the case of one of his neighbouring heads, who only:

> ... comes to one in five of our cluster heads' meetings, and he doesn't instigate ideas such as ... 'we'll have a shared training

day because there's no point in us doing them separately'. Other schools will organize that, and sometimes they'll join in, sometimes not. And then we do things like moderation across the cluster, so everyone takes an example of a level three piece of work to the Key Stage 2 meeting ... You know we do all that stuff, but three heads within the cluster do all the hosting and organizing and emailing round. And then others join in and come along to it, but haven't put the work in, so when it comes to doing ... thinking about maths and so on, we're reluctant to align ourselves with schools that we know are going to be passengers rather than drivers.

Being rural raises its own, different problems for capacity. As Arthur also pointed out: 'in a small school, you [just] haven't got time to go to meetings'.

At the opposite end of the spectrum, Marion, the head of a successful large primary school in London (in consultation to become five forms of entry, or over a thousand children eventually, in response to local demographic pressures) was also the head of a teaching school. It had agreed to take over the CPD programme from the LA 'where for example traditionally the schools had worked in isolation' with their NQTs. She compared this unfavourably with a neighbouring borough and described how she had 'had to sort out her own support' when she started as a new head there.

Joint practice development was, Marion said, fundamental to 'keeping standards high with so many more children'; they could not be allowed to dip because that would also threaten the teaching school status. This meant running a leadership team with two deputies and two assistants and all staff involved in faculties of about twenty members. The school was organized, until the age of 11, around the strands of the Early Years Foundation Stage (which in England precedes Key Stage 1), so there was a huge capacity for school improvement.

The leadership team observed lessons but staff did not regard the observations as being 'done unto them', Marion said. They were 'confident practitioners', accustomed to observing and being observed. The school had focus groups made up of a range of staff on, for example, how pupil premium funding was being used. One area of best practice at her school was the specialist centre for maths that was designated for the borough on the basis of the school's results. Good practice would be shared, groups of staff would 'look at the children's books', and would ask 'what could they do differently?' back in their own classrooms and schools. Marion argued that, consequently, joint practice development did not have to be organized specifically, as 'teachers are positive about working collaboratively [because of] its positive impact on their own practice'. They regarded it as a normal part of working together.

Marion had just stepped down as executive head of a neighbouring school as well, now that it was at the stage where it could offer some of its own expertise, for example, on the moderation of children's work. Competition was not a major issue here because of the expanding population. And, interestingly, after the two-school partnership, she still saw the LA area as the unit of loyalty, or at least the relevant sphere for professional working. This London borough, judging by this and other data, did seem to have enabled a transition to more school-led arrangements. Like Alison, Marion had found that, as the Teaching School, they were 'being approached more by schools because the LA advisers no longer had the capacity to provide support' though they were still 'proactive in signposting headteachers to where they could find the best support'. This is what a local school-led system could look like. It might also be why this school had no intention of seeking academy status but wished to remain a community school.

By contrast, Matthew, the head of the only outstanding primary school in his town, had wished to work mainly with the town's cluster of schools, perhaps due to the geographical possibilities or tribalism that Hargreaves mentions. But collaboration was not yet established there. Anyway, Matthew was clear that he could work with them only if there were 'tangible benefits for teaching and learning in my own school'. In the current absence of local collaborative work, he had sought more formal work as an LLE that was spread over a much wider group of schools. He described it from the point of view of establishing the sort of trust that Hargreaves considered the basis of long-term partnerships. Even though he was usually involved as a consequence of an RI judgement, he did not think 'it was helpful to look at Ofsted and what was wrong', always. Ultimately, he said, it was all about 'getting to good', but to work well support had to take into account the broader trajectory of the school, to 'look at the picture in the round [and] decide what you want to work on'. The two school teams had to be happy with one another.

His deputy acted up for him too when he was not available, but this was 'not a big ask' because of the professional development gained by that person. And the deputy head and other staff were involved in development work, for example, by leading so-called triads. As discussed earlier, three teachers would meet across the two schools and in turn be involved in three lessons together, possibly in English and maths, though it could be 'anything'. They would review the objectives together, plan the lesson, teach it, observe and then discuss it afterwards. His deputy would also lead staff meetings at the other school on a variety of topics. So again we see emerging elements of a school-led system rooted in joint practice development.

In another unitary authority, Jack's school had a wide variety of links with other schools – a relationship of 'polygamy', to use his term – even though it had just joined Donald's academy chain. Such links involved data-sharing through RAISEonline with primary schools not in the chain, peer-to-peer visits with six different schools and leadership links with schools in two other towns further away. He commented, however, that 'autonomy takes heads away from the classroom ... [And] operational freedom ... draws leaders away from teaching and learning'. In his own school, he had created time for middle leaders to focus on pedagogy, enabling them to pilot work and develop particular skills among students. They were replacing observations with 15-minute drop-ins into every classroom each week, but also asked the teachers to produce for review, each year, three films of lessons they thought were good, using the school's installed recording system.

Well acquainted with the notions of joint practice development, Jack did not believe voluntary partnerships 'allowed of any depth' in the work. He had also observed, he said, a Teaching School Alliance in a neighbouring authority quickly reaching capacity while servicing a small number of schools, even with 'a strategic deployment of NLEs and LLEs'. He saw being in the academy chain as a more structured way of allowing for such depth, making it possible to release him and his deputy to concentrate on improving the quality of teaching in their own school (the main reason the judgement on the school had slipped to RI, although the leadership was deemed good). Capacity is the key issue here too – what should leaders spend their time on?

Finally and notably, primary academy head Andrew had his own key to success. He described the path his school had taken to its current Ofsted status of 'Outstanding'. It had entailed:

> ... five years' hard graft to be able to get [my school) from 'requires improvement' through to 'outstanding'. And it's interesting being a junior school; you can take a number of different options, a number of different routes because you're a single-phase school. And we took one particular path and focused on the quality of teaching and formative assessment ... And we mapped it out in ten steps – ten steps! We just sat down and worked it out, myself and my deputy ... ten steps to get it from an RI, from satisfactory,

through to being outstanding. And if you do that, nine times out of ten it will get you to outstanding, I promise you that!

School development clustering

One of the LAs I visited for this research had pioneered the development of 'learning communities' as the basis for the school-to-school partnerships discussed here. They were grouped geographically, which, according to Leonard, an ex-primary head in the area and now a cluster coordinator:

> ... started off many years ago on an informal, less formal, basis, as cluster groups, without, and I would go right back to the 1980s ... really having ... the clear direction that many of them have now. And they met informally perhaps once a half term and exchanged thoughts and views in terms of a group of local schools.

These clusters were the sort of grouping described by Arthur. In this metropolitan area there were seven, formed from over eighty primary schools associated with seven secondary schools. The strategic intention of the LA, according to Charles, a senior LA officer, had been to:

> ... help launch our learning communities of schools ... from being clusters of schools that simply worked together, into a group that would have a learning community director. So we funded for two years all seven of our learning communities to have a community director who would lead on bringing them together, whether it be on a commercial basis for purchasing, or on an educational basis to deliver some key aspects.

The LA pump-primed what it called 'hub schools' within each learning community for two years. They had been developed to take a lead in a particular curriculum areas: literacy, numeracy, IT, early years or another specific locally identified area of expertise. For primary schools, the funding was £5,000 for two years. Three secondary schools were funded with £50,000 each to take a cross-borough lead in English, maths and science.

At the end of the two-year period, Charles said:

> ... it was up to the schools then, whether it would carry on or wither on the vine, depending on how well they'd used each other. And in a lot of cases it set schools up to be in a good position to become Teaching Schools, because now we've got nine Teaching Schools in the borough.

These developments had helped the Teaching Schools develop into being outstanding in Ofsted terms, creating 'a lot of capacity [for] when we have schools going into 'Requires Improvement' … for them to pick up from and get support'. The LA had commenced these developments after 'seeing the writing on the wall with the funding as it developed, [so this] had to be the catalyst. We always said to our headteachers, "we're here to work ourselves out of a job". And they improve schools, not us'.

The heads described some of the work of these learning communities:

> They vary from one learning community to another. Certainly the one that I'm involved in at present … is a fairly effective self-help group and we have meetings each half term. We have a range of events going on during the half term, and within the meetings in terms of standing items, that schools tap into as they see fits their needs.

The great advantage of these arrangements, according to Andrew, who as head of a primary academy compared his experience in a neighbouring authority, was that the heads had 'some sort of commonality. You had the same issues, you had the same problems, you had the same things that you wanted to be able to talk about'. The meetings had developed from 'basically a session where people just sat around moaning about the LA, with the LA adviser there', to becoming:

> … a powerful way of linking work that goes on, because we all have school improvement plans, we all have things we want to focus on …You still want to focus on what's the most important thing, which is the teaching and learning that goes on in your own individual schools and classes … and those life expectations that you can give with a good education to the children in [our area] of high deprivation – like most of [the LA] really.

For Andrew, investment was about 'getting that commonality and consistency' in the schools' discussions about teaching and learning:

> People will only buy into it if they see some sort of impact that it's going to have, to a point now where we've got specific frames of work that we're doing that we're prepared to pay money into … We're looking at trying to formalize it [learning community provision] a lot more through some of the work that we're doing.

The annual development plan of this learning community includes work to develop 'a collaborative school improvement programme', to include work on annual performance appraisals, phonics training and raising standards in SPAG, underpinned by a common coaching and mentoring system and a development programme for senior and middle managers. The learning community also has major pieces of work on attendance and safeguarding.

Andrew described how this learning community had set up joint training days with a focus on formative assessment and 'the impact it has upon the quality of teaching and learning'. Another important focus of interest, put together after the heads made suggestions to the coordinator while 'sitting round the table', was transition from primary to secondary school.

According to the documents I saw from one of the other learning communities elsewhere in the borough, the approach to development is different. Here there is one overall development plan, with a focus on the further development of the leadership and management skills of heads and deputies, and those in what Charles called the curriculum 'hub' areas, with each led by a specific primary school. The community had a focus on the development of accessible directories of good practice and 'outstanding teachers' – I have copies of these – for schools to access.

Another focus was on headteacher-led discussion of 'areas of interest', as Leonard said. These discussions were held at half-termly meetings attended by all the heads and sometimes their deputies. Here the host head was expected to 'talk to half a dozen bullet points' on either an area of strength or one the school was seeking to develop, after which other heads would describe how they had developed the same area.

With the end of LA pump-priming, however, finding capacity became more difficult. The 'elephant in the room', as Andrew called it, was money, hence his earlier 'buy into' comment. Pragmatic ways of creating capacity for secondary SLEs were noted earlier, but this is not currently possible for all schools. This affects the mechanisms available for sharing or jointly developing practice. Leonard's learning community had also developed half-termly learning walks: schools invite other heads into school for a morning, 'with a clear lead focus' introduced by the host headteacher. Visitors then spend time in the school to see how the focus is embedded in practice.

Leonard's learning community appears to have developed the stimulus for schools to seek advice and support from within the community, using the directories of good practice. The community had become the 'first port of call' for development needs, as he described it. It would require further research to determine whether the systematic relationships are being built between classroom teachers in different schools, as recommended by Hargreaves for mature partnerships. Clearly the basis for it exists here. But Andrew – and probably others – thought that it was inappropriate not to have the best teachers in front of their classes in a school serving a deprived area. The learning walks in Leonard's learning community were one response.

It had not been like this before. Ten years ago, Leonard was running a 'fresh start' school that became one of only two outstanding schools in the authority. His school received National College accreditation for the National Professional Qualification for Headship (NPQH) and hosted three-hour visits from deputies from all over the Midlands, though few from local schools. Similarly, when Andrew's school achieved outstanding status after implementing his 'ten steps' approach perhaps he too received visits from far afield in pursuit of the 'magic bullet' for junior schools. Few were outstanding at that time, but if there were a bullet, he said it would (merely!) be:

> ... about good quality teaching going on day in, day out, and [the head] making sure it happens to that level every single day. And it's easy to say that – damn difficult to get it.

This is a useful observation to apply as this book draws its conclusions: if this is what is required to address equity, then what will help bring more of it about? The arrangements in this urban area, with its mix of maintained and academy heads in the learning communities, are the basis for developing a school-led system, but there is more work yet to be done. Such arrangements were not so developed in any of the seven other LA areas I visited or interviewed in. There I learned of heads discussing building and sustaining good relationships with neighbouring schools and meeting regularly, sometimes holding such events as joint maths days (for example in Arthur's LA). But none reported the richness of discussion about classroom practice that this borough seems to have enabled. Nor does this seem to be replicated in LAs more widely, judging by research studies undertaken, even (or perhaps especially) where effort has been put into building LA-wide partnerships as a priority.

Given the mix of school-to-school work and experience I describe and the multiple partnerships some heads have formed, it is significant that the primary heads opt for working with schools nearby. This geographical relationship is identified by Hargreaves (2012b) as the safest basis for long-term partnerships based on trust.

The learning communities have to work somewhat differently with their secondary schools. Some of the successful secondary school partnerships described earlier are complicated in the ways schools relate with one another. Wherever I have travelled for this book and in my decades as an LA officer, I have found that schools belong to various clubs. This is a strategic issue. In an urban area, even transition is complicated; however broadly a cluster of primary schools is focused, secondary schools draw from a wider group still. One of the academies whose head I interviewed (Peter) draws its Year 7 from up to 30 primary schools each year – and this was not the most popular school with parents in his area.

But the secondary schools in this borough are also in the learning communities. The heads I interviewed were very positive about them: 'they're a great thing to have', as Peter said, after explaining the complications in deciding which one his school should belong to. But this NLE regarded them – rightly it seems – as principally focused on primary schools and their joint development, which the secondary heads recognized as being in their own long-term interest. Here we see another echo of Hargreaves' collective moral purpose. But the secondary heads, although contributing financially and sometimes in staff time to their own learning communities, did not think they got much out of them for their own schools' development. We saw that Michael's school was considering a multi-academy trust with his local primary schools as a surer foundation for 'making an impact in an area' and managing teaching and learning transition more effectively.

There is clearly more research to do to obtain a complete picture of what is happening. This is a school-led system-in-development, but with obvious signs of what such a system might look like. The question now is how this will emerge from the system it is replacing.

Chapter 6

Changing governance, realigning relationships: Emerging arrangements for a school-led system

We are the champion for all children, whether in an academy school or whether they're in a maintained school ... we have elected members running this council, who are responsible for what's happening in [the county], including what's happening to children in terms of their education, so I do see it as accountability. But I think it's more than that ... because schools don't operate [in] vacuums. And what happens in a school to children is directly related to what happens to them in a community. And also the idea that schools ... are free from LA control, do their own thing, while a significant number of those children will be being worked with, or their families, by the LA in a range of other ways, whether it's a child protection plan or a CAF [Common Assessment Framework] or an anti-social behaviour order, or the parents will be involved in whatever it is ... is not right. To try to pretend that that a school can operate as if it's unconnected to anything else, is, in my view, a real disservice to the children and the families.

(Catherine, chief officer, shire county, 2014)

LAs should also embrace a stronger role in education – not as providers of school improvement services but as guardians and champions of the needs and interests of all children in the area ... over a period of three years, LAs should phase out all their own provision of school improvement services and devolve them to school-led partnerships.

(Academies Commission, 2013: 7)

I have been surprised at how quickly the structural changes have taken place and the popularity of Teaching Schools. The [previous] secretary of state attempt[ed] to bypass LAs at every opportunity. His approach to school improvement was saying 'over to you' [schools] and clipping our [LAs'] wings.

(Douglas, senior local adviser and Ofsted inspector)

In terms of the LA, there is no real schools support there at all to speak of ... We're all on friendly terms, [but] in terms of school improvement ... there was never much there to be honest ... maybe a day a year ... But now it's gone and my perception of this seems to be that that the top tier is going to hang on to itself in the LA and a lot of the middle tier has been stripped away. The LA's got next to nothing to offer you know ... [I expect there to be] a realignment of clustering as LAs kind of fall away ... That's the way I see it, and ... it's not a case (now) of

every man for himself, but it's a case of: you've got to have a strategic sharpness and you've got to, you know, be strategically canny.
(Richard, headteacher, maintained faith secondary school)

The other elephant in the room

Inevitably, the developing and future role of the LA featured in many discussions, even when a question about it had yet to be asked. This was apparent in interviews with heads of maintained schools, academies and the free school, Ofsted inspectors, private sector consultants, heads of academy chains and the then current inspection providers, as well as LA officers across various levels of seniority and experience.

It is not clear at the time of writing whether the DfE pronouncement on the statutory responsibilities of LAs towards all schools, including academies (DfE, 2014b), settled the matter once and for all and to the satisfaction of everyone. And this pronouncement predated the legislation announced after the 2015 election.

Even after this 'clarification', LA officers were still considering the implications of their stated role of championing children and families, eloquently expressed by the chief officer quoted earlier, for when they had concerns about pupil outcomes or access in academies and free schools. I have tried to demonstrate that the articulation of the championing role had been developing in government circulars since the mid-2000s as a *counterbalance* – not necessarily deliberate – to the falling-away of direct involvement in school improvement. The commission on academies convened by the RSA (Academies Commission, 2013) made a similar articulation – as above.

The Local Government Association (LGA), in its manifesto for the 2015 general election (LGA, 2014a) advocated the championing role but also the merging of education funding bodies (for example the Education Funding Agency and councils). It wished to see councils' 'power to challenge' academies and free schools extended and local trusts set up for all schools, so that *all* 'headteachers and governors [can be] supported and held to account by councils' (*ibid*: 12). Both this manifesto and the earlier LGA document on 'rewiring public services' (2013) advocated the end of ring-fenced school budgets so that 'parts of this funding could more effectively spent on council services such as early intervention for vulnerable children' (LGA, 2014a: 21). This latter document makes little, overall, of the role of schools – perhaps an indicator in itself of the current state of change. While advocating 'renewing civic education' (*ibid*: 16) and 'putting school-leavers' work readiness higher up educational priorities' (*ibid*: 12) because 'employers have chosen not to hire the graduates of our schools and colleges' (*ibid*: 5), the document is silent on whether schools – as separate from children's services – are part of the transformation in public services the LGA seeks.

LAs do still have responsibilities with respect to all schools. I argue in my conclusion that there could be other responsibilities they should consider – helping build long-term school partnerships based on trust and supporting the development of local visions, especially in areas of deprivation. I echo the LGA (2014a) in this latter regard. LA involvement in such matters might be welcomed by headteachers. As I set out the remaining interview data in this chapter, I argue that however the as-yet-incomplete change is received by different actors, history has moved on as far as the *attitudes* of primary and secondary headteachers towards LAs are concerned. Whether or not they regret this, as some do, they are seeking to accommodate themselves and their schools to the developing new polity.

Change has been accelerated by two major factors. The first is the substantial budget cuts to LAs. Over the lifetime of the 2010–15 Parliament, councils were asked to prepare 40 per cent cuts in their expenditure because of cuts in central government grant (LGA, 2014b). According to the LGA, these would not have been complete everywhere by the time of the 2015 election as councils were affected differently and were using their accumulated reserves in various ways. Nevertheless, council finances are unsustainable in the long term (LGA, 2014a) and it is not clear how the new government's comprehensive spending review will affect them further.

Many councils – although not all – had undertaken a major review of their education functions and strategy concomitantly to help them make the cuts. As Charles said: 'budget cuts make you more strategic, don't they?' His council undertook a strategic education review in 2010, consulting the schools. It reduced the net budget for its services to schools by over 80 per cent, transferring staff to an organization separate from the council that had to earn its entire income by charging schools for services, not just in the LA's own area but increasingly in surrounding areas as the business developed.

The second major factor to speed up change was the expansion of the academy programme. The nature of academy status has changed the dynamic between such schools and some LAs, sometimes dramatically, affecting how the council conceives its role. This has undoubtedly been exacerbated by the developing regional state. As noted, becoming an academy and ceasing to be a maintained school means that the converted school receives a share of the LA central budget for services deemed to be provided for it when it was a maintained school. Most of the officers interviewed reported budget changes because of this, but also said their central council departmental budgets – such as that of the chief executive – had often escaped taking a share of the reductions.

The headteachers expressed their views about conversion to academy status and their opinions of LA services and what their role might be. I will set these out here before exploring the LAs' strategic work in supporting school-to-school networking and setting up LA-wide partnerships. Finally in this chapter I consider the perceived legitimacy of LAs – professional, community and democratic. But first I examine a spread of studies that set the interview data in context.

Becoming an academy

Some of the schools I visited had been academies for some time. Few of the heads I interviewed had seen academy status as an escape from the LA, but some did. Peter, as head of an early converter, had a long litany of complaints:

> ... if I am honest, local authority frustration was, and had been, a big issue for us. For example, the local authority at one point wished to close our school. So you have a school here which was really succeeding, jewel in the crown, the only outstanding school in [the LA] and you want to close it and move it to another part of the borough which has falling rolls, a very poor school and they wanted to move us there. It was all political basically ... you know, local council politics.

This is not the first or last school to seek to escape an LA strategic review or seek better resource allocations. Some of the first grant-maintained schools were formed for just these reasons (Fitz *et al.,* 1993) and determined much of my own experience as a senior LA officer at that time. Peter had other concerns:

> And the local authority even now does not tend to support schools, in my view ... and we tend to say 'can you actually work with us, rather than having to battle with us?'

He raised a number of what were clearly long-running issues, such as closing the road that separated some of the school's buildings, the funding allocated under Building Schools for the Future (a capital funding scheme scrapped by the Coalition Government when it came to power in 2010), the annualized payments for the borough's PFI (private finance initiative) scheme that arose as a consequence, top slices of their funding being used to finance developments elsewhere in the LA and the single day a year of support the council could offer the school (which is not unusual now). This led the staff and governors to ask, according to Peter, 'what is the point of us being here ... having this conversation? ... [So] we questioned the value of being part of this organization'.

With this head's consent, I informed the LA of these complaints. I have been unable to assemble some comparable national figures for PFI payments. They vary according to which extra services are included in the contract with the private sector *special purpose vehicle* set up to manage it, be it cleaning, grounds maintenance or, sometimes, some teaching costs. But the reported £1.2 million a year from an annual budget of £9 million did seem high to me. Martin, another secondary headteacher (of a maintained school in the same LA) made similar complaints about the size of the payments, though he was very pleased with the new buildings. And understandably so – I was acquainted with the old ones. Also, any complaints elsewhere in the country about PFI – not sought in the interviews – tended to be more about the construction of the contract. For example, schools were grouped together in one scheme in the shire county but they were now seeking different destinies.

The conversation between Peter's school and the LA had assumed an unhelpful tone I did not encounter elsewhere. But the comment about the lack of any services from the LA was common, and not just for secondary schools. As well as Peter's there is the comment from Richard at the top of this chapter and that from Thomas at the top of Chapter 4.

The comments from academy heads were typically very pragmatic about converting. Thomas again:

> ... we've always been a relatively successful school, and the interventions and support we had from [the county] had been being phased out over a number of years. So they'd been reduced, so we were buying in some services, but we had already outsourced our HR and payroll and the bits of advice like that ... There were quite a few things we weren't buying, but we continued to buy some services ... welfare officers and various other bits and bobs. It didn't feel like it fundamentally changed the relationship for us ... We had already, if you like, been double-paying for some things that we were paying as part of the [county] settlement. But then we felt we were able to get a better local offer ...

Such comments make it seem as though academy status was the end of a natural process of development. Thomas specifically remarked that there was not 'a hugely ideological agenda with [the county] or the schools, it's been a very pragmatic one', echoing the policy approach of Simkins *et al.*'s 'county' in their research:

> ... which had been traditionally a low interventionist administration [attempting] to minimize the activity and impact of the local state by giving as much autonomy to schools as possible.
>
> <div align="right">(Simkins <i>et al.</i>, 2014: 6)</div>

This is the policy orientation of Catherine's council quoted at the top of this chapter. It wasn't always quite the same everywhere. Dominic, the head of an academy chain, talked about the view taken by the LA at the time he was first thinking of academy status for the school where he had been head (in 2011):

> ... a senior officer made it really clear that [they were] against the idea of academies and [were] going to make it difficult for us ... In one meeting it was said that ... the guns were to be wheeled out on to the lawn – which wasn't exactly top partnership speak! ... So you know we had to point out to [them] it wasn't actually [their] decision who we worked with in the new landscape.

This refers to a unitary authority in the South West. The comment is another that shows how matters progressed rapidly after 2010. Generally, though, the discussions that had taken place (and in many cases were to be resumed after the 2015 general election) did seem to be based on the many practical aspects of conversion, including the reduced extra money available. This might have been expected in the shire county. Thomas explained the history of grant-maintained status there over twenty years ago. His governors felt that, in not going grant-maintained then, they never:

> ... got anything much back from our offer of loyalty to the LA. So they saw the advantage which some neighbouring schools had in terms of the cash – those schools that first became grant-maintained really did get a lot of money out of the system. And that entrenched an advantage for them, by which, in the history ... the sort of, you know, cultural history of the school, we felt we never caught up with. Although ... we worked very closely with the [local schools] ... it was always felt that they had gained then and we hadn't. And therefore the governors, several of whom had been through that process, felt very strongly that when there was an opportunity for us to convert we needed to. Because if there

was any advantage in the system, any financing money, then we needed to get it quickly because it would disappear. And although it probably wasn't going to make us money it might just protect us a bit in leaner times. And that has been our experience: I mean we've, yeah … we've relied on that sum of money to provide a roll-over and as a cushion.

Especially, as Thomas explained, as the school (like many others and some of those I visited) was facing some tough financial years ahead with unfunded rises in national insurance and superannuation contributions, on the one hand, and the accumulating dramatic cuts in funding for post-16 places, on the other. For heads like Peter, beside the historic antagonism to the LA, cuts in funding for nationally agreed school specialisms also posed a potential recurrent funding problem of about half a million pounds, which the new status at that time helped them manage. The issue of cutbacks had also featured in the discussions with the staff prior to change.

Whatever the previous difficulties experienced by Dominic in relations with senior officers, he too described similarly pragmatic considerations about conversion:

You know for us it was never about not working with a local authority, and I would emphasize that every step of the way, that we still work really closely with the local authority on issues where we need to work with them. We buy some services from them, but a lot of services we didn't. And partly I think because at the point that we went, the different groups within [the authority] just hadn't realized what it was to have to pitch in an open market and they, if I'm blunt about it, they were clueless. So if I give you an example: the school's personnel team were absolutely desperate for us to buy services from them but they wanted us to buy payroll as well as a kind of HR support. But they wanted to charge us twice as much as anyone else in the market place and they couldn't see that that meant, in terms of best value, there was no way we were ever going to go with that. And I think, you know, they've refined what they do in the meantime, but … part of about being one of those early converters is … you've got a mindset in your organization … you're going to go out and find the best in order to create the capacity to do other things with the financial benefit that's there. There *was* a bit of financial benefit to start with, but that's long gone.

Arthur, the primary head, told me he had:

> ... obviously known about academies for some time now, as I always like to know what is going on, and I guess we started looking early on as to whether it would be useful for us. I've always looked at it from the point of view of what difference this would make to children within the school. And I also looked to colleagues across [the county] to see, you know, what they're doing, and ... there's not been anything that's made me think, 'this is going to make our school a lot better for children if we became an academy'. But things have recently shifted and I – because of what's going on very locally – I am looking closely, with a couple of colleagues from the same cluster – we're a small cluster – at how potentially we could become academies.

He explained that he and his colleague cluster heads 'had done lots of joint planning, and were just looking into the MATs [multi-academy trusts] at the moment' after a 'useful meeting' with an LA officer. Part of his concern was about wanting to take the step to academy status 'of our own accord' and avoid being forced to do so after a future poorer Ofsted verdict.

His counterpart in a unitary authority, Alison, explained in 2014 how they had examined academy status four years earlier after a new chair of governors was elected who was strongly in favour of it and had been involved in chains elsewhere in the country:

> So we ... had a whole year of looking into it ... and apart from [the chair] everybody voted against it at that time. Now, interestingly, nearly four years on I would say that we are in a different situation anyway and academies are in a different situation ... It's me that's looking at it a little bit more ... at the moment, although we have set up various meetings with various bodies, to look at maybe ... if we did this, what would it look like ... I think, from our point of view, we are a large expanding school; we're a lead school in many, many things ... [and] we are also constantly being got at by the diocese to consider becoming an academy ... So, possibly, we might look at something around the diocese [here].

Michael, another primary head, speaking in 2014, said he was thinking about it too, he and his staff being 'in a fortunate position to be masters of [their] own destinies'. He had had a discussion with the RSC about the potential system role of his school in the town and whether it should convert to facilitate this. This discussion too seemed to be essentially pragmatic, but his school had recently been instructed by the LA to admit an extra class in response to local demographic pressure. Michael talked at length about 'very, very unhelpful [LA] officers' not informing him of deadlines and said the LA admissions team had '[handled] the process very badly'. He was less negative about his LA overall than Peter, but he was clear that he would not have had to take the extra children if he had been an academy.

Jack, one of Michael's colleagues working in a different unitary authority, spoke favourably in 2015 about what his LA *had been like*. It had been 'collegiate', staffed with 'people with strong moral purpose', but was now, in his view, 'less strategic' and had been focused mainly on 'reaction to Ofsted for the past three years'. He had sought and achieved academy status to align the school with a local academy chain (Dominic's) in an area of long-standing collaboration among the heads. According to Dominic, the other primary school had also joined because its head:

> … would tell you that she has seen the move into the [academy chain] being about having extra support for her and her school that she felt wasn't there with the local authority and its dwindling resources.

The forces at work here – likely to be accelerated in the Conservative Government, possibly dramatically – are cumulative. The LA might have undertaken a strategic review, but it had to reduce its services because of budget cuts. This had meant the departure of particularly valued members of staff, often ex-primary heads or deputies, and this had especially worried the primary heads. Jack mentioned one person in particular.

Leonard and Andrew also spoke of the *personal nature* of headship: 'when you create a school you create it in your own image of what you feel education is about. It is everything about you [and] you drive the ethos. You drive the ethos, yes.' Their relationship with their SIA or SIP, whoever or whatever that might be – in one case it was the coordinator of a learning community – was consequently also intense and personal, specifically in the area of school improvement. Other services (payroll, human resources and even children's services), though still important, mattered less. Andrew gave a vivid example concerning a previous member of the LA's school improvement team: 'it was absolutely incredible the impact that he had within [our area] as a whole, let alone … that he had within my school'. He went on to say how different it was now and how different it had been in another LA where the service had been privatized after a national intervention. His comments in that regard were analogous to those made by Martin about 'PFI contract culture'.

We can see, then, that as valued members of LA staff left and were not replaced, the headteachers valued the LA *as a whole* less. And as more and more schools take up academy status, the capacity of the LA is further reduced, making it less likely that it will be able to provide new and valued members of staff with whom the heads can have a sustained relationship. In tandem with the processes running since 2005, they are beginning to seek their own new support staff. This is a further – and deliberate – motor behind the development of a school-led system. As Andrew, now head of an academy, observed, there is a sort of natural rhythm and pragmatic progression in response to these changes:

> You have to keep moving, because if you don't you'll get left behind ... really, and I think you have to as a headteacher. You have to be master of what you actually see; you know we're talking about vision, and ... what you want for your school, and what you want for the children that are coming to that school on a day-to-day basis ... but also for the long-term future. Now, if it means working for the LA, then that's fine, but you have to bear in mind that sometimes part of the LA, what it offers ... because of budget cuts, or because of the nature of what they're actually offering, there are other things out there. And I think it's just a natural move from local management of schools in the eighties ... and we're reaching that point now.

He went on to echo Catherine, quoted earlier:

> I'm not one of these academy heads who sees it as ... well, I'm going on me own. I am, technically speaking, but I think not all academies want ... to disengage totally from what the authority bring, because they are the overseers as far as the local community is concerned.

The heads of academy chains I interviewed may not be representative of all their colleagues, but they too mentioned the declining capacity of LA staff, although more to express their regret. James, as a head of the large chain, was actually an advocate of the LA championing role. Nevertheless, he said in 2013:

> I do think that local authorities have a very mixed record in school improvement. Local authorities weren't actually designed or set

up to do school improvement – that was a much later intervention. Structurally that's not quite how you do it I think, in an ideal way … [but anyway some] local authorities have stopped being providers of … secondary education in the area [and] I don't think they have the capacity to do school improvement in most cases any more, you know. Budget pressures have stopped that.

He was also saying, however, that LAs do have the capacity to 'provide the appropriate challenge', though Daniel regretfully disagreed:

So working closely with a local authority was just what I did and I felt quite passionate about that, so my desire to set up the [academy chain] was in no way a negative reaction to the local authority support, although … I'm sure we both know … there's very little quality work left in our local authorities now, but I, we, still play a part in that.

Dominic described how his chain was *de facto* undertaking the major school improvement role more and more in his part of the LA area with the LA's consent and sometimes at its initiative. This is a continually shifting story. Several Ofsted inspectors I interviewed, who also did pre- and post-Ofsted consultancy with schools, also talked about the 'varying picture' with respect to LA school improvement services. Jean, who worked for an Ofsted inspection provider, said that their inspection teams had noticed that in some LAs outsourcing had just been about saying 'get on with it' to another organization, and few of the people left knew much about the schools. Some LAs 'knew [next to] nothing' about their schools as a consequence, while in others, an experienced inspector told me, 'there [seems to be] a fair number of people floating around' and that some LAs were increasing their school improvement function.

The story emerging from these interviews is largely about pragmatic responses, with heads considering the benefits for their school and the wider likely changes in the polity. As noted, Marion, who had just stepped down as an executive head in London, told me she was certainly not considering academy status as every school near her in her area wished to remain a 'community school'. The move from an LA-driven role to an LA-wide partnership run by the headteachers, to which she said '95 per cent of the schools were signed up' seemed to be enough. Aside from the pragmatic matters heads consider, the influence of what is presented to them as possible, desirable and as the long-term shape of the polity in the national discourse cannot be discounted. The RSCs are promoting academy status as part of their job but as Alison, head of the Church of England school, said, her diocese and others were doing the same. And I was shown a copy of a detailed PowerPoint presentation prepared by a solicitor whose company was engaged by one of the churches to advise governing bodies on the decision-making structures that needed to be set up for academy status.

LAs and school improvement
Overall role
The final report on the role of LAs from the ISOS Partnership for the Ministerial Advisory Group (Parish *et al.,* 2012) identified the three functions of LAs as: ensuring a sufficient supply of school places; tackling underperformance in schools and ensuring high standards; and supporting vulnerable children. These headings were taken up by Smith *et al.*'s 'rapid review' on 'enabling a school-driven system' (2012). They vary slightly from the functions set out in *The Importance of Teaching* (DfE, 2010: 16).

These two reports are largely focused on the role of 'middle tier' organizations, that is, those situated somewhere between central government and schools. They take authority for their deliberations from the second McKinsey systems report (McKinsey, 2010) that found some organization played the middle tier role in all the successful schools systems they reviewed. The role is defined as ensuring effective channels of communication, facilitating conversations and partnerships and 'mediating' (Smith *et al.*, 2012: 6). The size and nature of the middle-tier organizations in the McKinsey report, however, vary widely.

None of this is really new. Michael Fullan has long advocated 'tri-level reform' (see 2003, for example), from the time of his original work in Ontario – also one of the systems reviewed by McKinsey. One purpose of the middle tier is to enable an informed, effective and ongoing conversation with, and between, school leaders about improvement set within the context of a local schools system. Simplifying this conversation was the point of the 'new relationship' with schools (DfES, 2004b) in the early 2000s, although even then these proposals reflected the developing move away from LAs, as noted. But the limitations inherent in the second role for LAs articulated by Parish *et al.* (2012) – tackling underperformance in schools and ensuring high standards – are illustrated by this comment from Richard, the head of an *outstanding* secondary school. His school, like most others, he says, does not always achieve a uniform upward trajectory in attainment outcomes:

> I can show you 12 years of data in headship and it's a mountain
> range, it's not a ski slope and it's … up and down. I've sat in this

> very office some August days on results day in a state of almost complete depression. I think how on earth did we get that figure, you know, and I've sat in here or gone in there clicking my heels ... you learn that there are ups and downs, and I suppose you develop a more even temperament. You don't get too excited on the good days and you don't get too down on the bad days ...

The focus in his school had always been on high standards and it had never been accused of underperformance. Yet, an ambition limited to 'ensuring high standards' will not provide the continuing motivation or encouragement to go on developing once high standards are achieved. Nor more generally for such schools to examine continually the outcomes achieved by their children: are they uneven between groups, for example, and if so what are the root causes?

Nationally the systemic pressure on English schools has been provided through floor targets and benchmarks such as that, set in 2012, for every school to be good or better in Ofsted terms. These are in enforced by Ofsted and backed up by intervention, increasingly now by the RSCs. Where the vast majority of schools have already achieved good or better (Ofsted, 2014b), such as Richard's, all that remains nationally to do for all schools is to ratchet up expectations again. How long can such a system endure with its changing standards, constant pressure and implied distrust of heads and their staff?

Something more and different is required for all schools. Every headteacher I interviewed understood the role of national expectations. But if internal school processes have to be kept in a state of permanent readiness for a brief, infrequent encounter with Ofsted inspectors who have little or no knowledge of the school, this makes it harder to develop the long-term professional classroom-to-classroom relationships based on trust, as advocated by Hargreaves (2012b). It has to take second place. Yet it is only in the depth, shared intelligence, reflectiveness and openness of such sustained peer-to-peer networks that schools may seek long-term answers to questions of equity, and students can continue to be motivated, stimulated and inspired to achieve more. We have seen the beginnings of such alternative relationships in the interview evidence.

There is no choice in this matter. Networks, learning communities, deep partnerships – or whatever we choose to call them – are needed for the long-term health of state schooling and teachers. The bazaar must replace the cathedral – the network the hierarchy – because the cathedral no longer works in current professional and social climates (Mason, 2015). It invites shallow responses and, against short-term targets, shallow understandings on the part of teachers. A new model for schools and the teaching profession is required. There needs to be a different conception of professional autonomy, framed within national expectations. There are also signs in the interview evidence that what could be seen as a new two-stage model is emerging.

For LAs, 'tackling underperformance in schools and ensuring high standards' could have been the basis for the school improvement work of councils in England, historically the principal middle tier. This would be but the first stage of a new model, usually interpreted in LA documents as identifying poor performance through their data-collection and brokering packages of support from the system leadership available within the school community (Parish *et al.*, 2012; Aston *et al.*, 2013). But, leaving aside variable LA performance, the expansion of the academies programme and budget cuts mean that some LAs are *de facto* not performing this for many or any schools, with some not even knowing where there are needs, as noted. With new legislation, LAs may shortly not do this work at all for any schools.

The complexity of how LAs provide for 'vulnerable children' – those who have special educational needs or a disability, children in the public care and a number of other groups – is beyond the scope of this book even though aspects of the work are about equity. Parish *et al.* (2012) interpret this work in a fairly limited way as being about fair access agreements – making sure these students are able to attain a suitable school place – and having access to appropriate services, important though both of these are. This reflects Julian's earlier comment about the now transactional nature (that is, transaction by transaction) of the relationship between secondary schools and their LAs on special educational needs.

The strategic planning required for school places is also beyond the scope of this book. Noting Julian's comments, I would argue that school improvement is at the very core of the struggle for equity and is so close to the hearts of headteachers that it affects their perception of the LA as a whole, beyond being just one service provider among many.

Data offer and monitoring

For the LAs this more limited stage one role first requires adequate data. All the officers I spoke to regarded their data offer to schools, and the risk assessment it enabled, as central to their role. For example, in the shire county, Catherine said:

> We have a system of collecting a range of different data – we
> have a very well-developed process for doing that – and then
> we aggregate the range of data, whether ... [on] attainment or
> progress, or the number of complaints, or exclusions. A whole
> range of data; we've got all of that identified. And then ... at
> regular intervals during the year we then take an oversight of that
> to look at any schools where there would appear to be concerns.

In this LA an annual review was available to the governing bodies of
schools, whether or not they were academies. The SIAs who are 'mostly
serving headteachers [and] not employed directly by the LA' undertake this
review and go to a school more often if it is causing concern. If the school
requires support they would be 'pointed in the right direction' (Catherine),
or 'signposted' as Marion said in a different context. Catherine's authority
prioritizes its 'resources to focus on those most in need in terms of our
brokerage'. This is about 'putting schools in touch with each other'. If
possible this will be quality-assured, but doing so was not always possible
as Catherine said frankly:

> We would expect the school that was receiving that support to
> decide [on its quality]. We might be giving advice, but we don't
> have the capacity to be monitoring ... [or] quality-assuring every
> bit of support that's happening. It is meant to be a sector-led
> system ... We just simply don't have the capacity.

Moreover:

> If it was a school that was outstanding then, and it was maintained,
> then they would never see us unless we were going to ask them to
> go and work with another school.

This shire county puts schools into categories on the basis of this broad
range of data. Catherine again: 'we're very clear with schools that we
categorize them, and we say, these are the criteria for which category you're
going to be in'. And 'depending on the category that schools are in, that will
determine how much interface there [is] with the council'.

This shire did not publish the criteria more generally, however, unlike
the more hands-on urban council where Charles is a senior officer – and as
anticipated by Simkins *et al.*, 2014 – although there are many similarities.
Charles explained:

> The biggest driver for us was the way in which we shared data
> with schools ... Because this is ... a deprived authority in terms

of the makeup of the folk here; people were using that as an excuse ten years ago for performance. So what we did is we took our whole ... spread of abilities, used the IDACI indicators [see Chapter 1] and then ranked all the schools on a sort of quadrant graph of IDACI performance against outcomes, to demonstrate ... that three of these primary schools were out-performing the schools in better areas. We only have, in the whole borough ... two schools above the national average for IDACI; everybody else is ... in the very bottom quartile.

So what we then did is we took our quartiles and we created our own league tables and initially schools hated it: four columns for the quartiles we had, so ... this was developed into the IDACI columns ... and then we were able to demonstrate against that performance, naturally across, so that schools could actually see that the schools in the bottom quartile, if they had good leadership and management, were out-performing schools at the top.

This approach seemed to be successful:

The year after we published it we had a sort of 5 per cent increase, so we published it again. Another 5 per cent increase on results [followed]. And that happened for about three years in a row because we were sharing it and schools were happy to see it ... And what it did, it helped, it flushed out schools in the middle sectors that were coasting as well as those [that] were really seriously underperforming.

Charles said that until 2010 this LA had an annual 'conversation' with the head and chair of governors of every school at the council's HQ. This might involve up to 20 officers – the gatherers of the data across the council referred to by Catherine – and it helped establish 'performance management of [school] staff and ... [made our] understanding [of] the schools better'. At that stage, Charles said, '90 per cent of the schools would enjoy the conversation and 10 per cent wouldn't'. These 'conversations', based on data available to all, have been reduced, however, as in Catherine's county, to being 'just [taking place with] the schools we're highly concerned about, because we know the others are doing it'.

This again is in line with national expectations. A difference in the urban authority is that it still has a large primary school improvement adviser team (eight full-time equivalents) of whom four are headteachers bought in for a certain number of days each year, with three for secondary bought in similarly. In this proactive LA this reduction in school observation raises a concern for Charles about:

> ... the quality of what happens in schools. If we're not monitoring it, you only have to look at ... [he refers to two large nearby LAs, both of which had attracted severe recent criticism] ... who have been unable to get into their schools more than once a year ... You cannot judge quality by only going into a school once a year, or looking at results once a year ... It's simply just to make sure we're on top of it.

Some of this data-gathering can therefore be characterized as a desktop review discussed once a year with some schools – but not all – and on a basis to be decided by the schools. The other LAs reported some version of what has been described. It is not possible to determine how representative these data are, but it seems reasonable to assume that all LA provision could be characterized as falling somewhere on the spectrum between this latter authority with a 'traditionally ... interventionist administration', on the one hand, and the 'traditionally ... low interventionist administration' of the shire county (Simkins *et al.*, 2014: 6), on the other. But 'knowing the schools' is crucially important for both ends.

Unfinished work: The limits of LA roles

All 59 LAs that responded to an ADCS-commissioned survey said they 'wish[ed] to continue to have a lead role in addressing the issues of schools causing concern' (Pritchard, 2012: 2). A number of the studies commissioned as part of the review by the National Foundation for Educational Research (NFER) entitled *What Works in Enabling School Improvement? The role of the middle tier'* (Aston *et al.*, 2013) claim further that the 'Chief Inspector of Schools stated ... in his ... Annual Report ... [that] it is part of LAs' responsibility to promote improvement in all ... schools, including academies' (Crossley-Holland, 2013b: 2). This claim has continued to animate officers' statements (Crossley-Holland, 2012), the LGA (2013; 2014a) and Catherine, the chief officer quoted at the top of this chapter. Ofsted stated that:

> Local authorities continue to hold a democratic accountability for securing good outcomes for all children and young people in a local area and a statutory duty in exercising their education and training functions to do so with a view to promote high standards and promote the fulfilment of learning potential.
>
> (Ofsted, 2012: 16)

The question for LAs, as is the case for any interpretation of quasi-legal wording, is: what can be, or needs to be, meant by 'securing' and 'promote' in this connection, in the light of earlier discussions? Clarity is especially needed because the statement has been used as the basis for Ofsted's judgements of LAs, taking as a starting point the percentage of children in their respective areas that attend 'good' or 'better' schools compared with the national average figures.

But although many if not most academy headteachers bore no antagonism towards their LAs, for most it just no longer featured in their stated wider work horizons for school improvement. It did feature, however, where the LA retained statutory responsibility for children who have special educational needs or disabilities ('supporting vulnerable children'). Even then, secondary heads had a string of complaints where their LA was trying to reconfigure joint working or geographical co-location for children's services. Thomas complained about not being treated as a full partner; and Jack said it was 'hard to see what the plan was' for partnership but he actually meant overall, too. Secondary heads in particular complained about the 'we know best' attitude of some LA staff – the social workers, service managers and youth workers where they still existed. But the LGA (2014a) had said the ring-fencing of school budgets should be ended so that the money could be spent on LA services.

Further, some of the academy heads were unaware of the data offer, or that their LA offered an annual event or review. Because of the routine nature of data management in the lives of schools today, this may have been because it was dealt with by school data managers, some of whom are assistant or deputy heads or business managers. There is no unambiguous evidence on this matter at this stage of the development of the polity – it seems everyone will have a different story.

Julian, the private sector consultant, was of the opinion that the LA data offer was still valued by schools, and one of the future RSCs I interviewed commented that the new regional teams would work closely with LAs and use their data. But they would also have access to their own from the DfE, as would Ofsted through their annual risk assessments – another desktop review. A lot of data have also been available to all schools for some time, for example, by school or LA subscription through the Fisher Family Trust, or RAISEonline, originally commissioned by the DfE's predecessor and Ofsted from RM Data. So some schools at least, speaking more broadly, may just not use the LA service because there is so much data available elsewhere.

Out of interest, and as a footnote to trying to determine where schools may be sourcing their data, I emailed two academy heads I had interviewed in different authorities to ask if they would share their LA data. Both did so by return. For the secondary school, the useful data included what was described as a 'first flush' data set, intended to provide data in the LA area for the current year that were as yet unpublished. For the primary school, its unitary authority provided an extremely detailed data profile, including data for attendance, early years foundation stage outcomes, phonics and Key Stages 1 and 2 data. The introduction to this profile expressed the intention to 'monitor and improve the choice of the indicators year on year so the profile becomes a more integrated data system relating to the school's self-evaluation needs'. That itself is an important piece of work for both improvement and preparation for Ofsted inspection. In addition, the profile says, 'the school will need to have a plan for how it manages and uses this profile and other information', naming RAISEonline as one such option. So if there is to be a conclusion on this, it is that schools pull together their outcome data themselves, using LA data as they see fit.

To return to interpretations of 'promote' and 'secure': if an LA has a concern about an academy, based on data from across the council, it can raise it directly with the school's governing body. In the shire county, this was welcomed in a high profile case, Catherine, the chief officer, told me. In a nearby unitary authority, however, Adrian, a proactive, committed and locally well-regarded chief officer, raised a series of concerns with the governing body of a local academy, but with no response. When the same complaints were raised with the Secretary of State, there was again no response and the matter was referred to the Education Funding Agency. I cannot give more detail without identifying the school and LA, but one Ofsted inspector I interviewed was well aware of the case and thought it unlikely to happen now, since the 'appointment of the Regional Schools Commissioners'. He gave some examples from his experience of wider issues with academies, however, such as when they did not accept Ofsted judgements.

Overall, LAs can now invite academies and free schools to join their partnership arrangements, where they exist, and then raise any data-driven concerns (including access) through the RSCs after the school governing body. But Adrian, in an impassioned follow-up email to me (in 2014), expressed the view that:

> The power lies predominantly [in such situations] with the suppliers [schools] and this combined with a potential accountability

vacuum [where the academy is ... good or outstanding] can leave parents in an untenable position with no authoritative advocate able to force an academy to act reasonably.

He went on to say that the 'evolving system is skewed towards the suppliers'. This puts both the word 'promote' and the more general championing role in a different light.

LA partnerships

Many but not all LAs have been, and are, engaged in efforts to set up new forms of partnership between themselves and the schools in their areas. Their developing strategic vision is informed by a 'commitment to enabling schools, irrespective of their status, to lead their own improvement', according to Parish *et al.* (2012: 4) and the national policy direction. This action research report into the 'evolving role of the LA in education' (*ibid.*) examined 'LAs as convenors of partnerships' (*ibid*: 39 onwards). These were not all focused on school improvement, but included their work under the two other functions as well. The ones that were focusing on some form of school-to-school partnership working for school improvement included Kingston, Richmond, Bristol, Gloucestershire, Bolton, East Sussex, Warwickshire and Hertfordshire.

Five developed or developing LA partnership arrangements were reviewed in detail for the NFER's *What Works* report (Aston *et al.*, 2013). These were York (Crossley, 2013a), Wigan (Crossley, 2013b), Brighton and Hove (Crossley-Holland, 2013a), Hertfordshire (Crossley-Holland, 2013b) and Southend (Crossley-Holland, 2013c).

In addition, the Local Government Association, with the Chief Executive's Association, SOLACE, published *The Council Role in School Improvement* (LGA/SOLACE, 2013). This reviewed a variety of activities, some more about partnership *working* than the actual partnerships, in Dorset, East Sussex, Lambeth, Leicester, Devon, Hertfordshire, Kingston, Solihull, Wigan, Durham, Ealing, Liverpool, Gloucestershire, Camden, Suffolk, Bexley, Brighton and Hove and Sunderland.

Finally, Richard Hatcher (2014) published his own review of the partnership arrangements in Birmingham, drawing on some of the above research. The added merit of Hatcher's work is that it charts critically some of the developing relationships over time between the city's headteachers and the City Council, analysing their significance.

All these featured case studies make interesting reading, with most of the authorities having mixed economies but differing balances of academies, free schools and maintained schools. These were represented differently on the various partnership bodies. One LA, Oxfordshire, had decided to encourage all its schools to convert to academy status; Catherine's shire county was neutral on the issue, regarding it as a matter for the schools.

The arrangements surveyed over all these publications cover a range of authorities, pointing to perhaps more representative conclusions, though they are all reporting on what was in place two or three years ago when change was rapid. This makes a comparative analysis of their functions and work somewhat otiose, especially with new legislation announced. To understand what is happening now and theorize its significance, further surveys and research need to be undertaken from time to time.

In addition, the publications in which the LGA is involved, partly no doubt because of the inchoate nature of some of the arrangements being described at that time, are very much studies of local government *intentionality*, subject to the complexities of realization discussed earlier. What is the point of having a so-called vision, for example, if no one pays it any attention? Really importantly, some analysis is needed of the *depth* of school partnerships, and whether this can enable school-to-school support of the bazaar nature (stage two of the professional model I argue for). None of these publications does this and the present book does not have sufficient local data either. More in-depth case studies are needed.

Nevertheless, many of the arrangements deal in different ways with a common series of tasks and issues with respect to 'promoting' school improvement, in Parish *et al.*'s formulation (2012), some also as defined by Hargreaves (2012b). One such issue had been, after the publication of the Coalition White Paper (DfE, 2010b), what to do with some very large LA school improvement services in the light of changing roles and budget cuts. As we saw, one solution was outsourcing either to a private sector company (for instance Babcock's in the case of two shire counties) or a special arm's-length body created for the purpose (the metropolitan borough I visited), both of which would be able to charge for their services. Hertfordshire had done this fairly early on; so had Richmond.

Building system capacity was to be done through helping recruit more NLEs, LLEs and SLEs, though none of the studies identifies whether this was likely to be successful (for example, in Kingston). Another matter was *deciding* how and when this system leadership or other support and development resources should be deployed. One authority, Bolton, was setting up an electronic resource directory, although, as Catherine noted, it is difficult to go on guaranteeing a quality-assurance role in a changing market except on the basis of 'TripAdvisor-type' comments from schools, as the LA with its diminishing resources is likely to know less and less about independent providers. Some partnerships *seemed* to be deploying capacity via the LA-wide partnership (Brighton and Hove; Wigan), sometimes by commissioning work from a local Teaching School or Teaching School Alliance. Elsewhere, as Hatcher (2014) says, some headteachers preferred to do this directly, sometimes even in an LA that had a partnership.

Such deployments are supposed to be made in response to identified need – the intervention aspect of the school improvement function – so largely after an Ofsted judgement or data-identified risk. At least at stage one of the model. Some partnerships were dealing with data, particularly the risk-based allocations of schools to categories as described by Charles using IDACI data. Some developing partnerships, such as in one of the unitary authorities I visited, were intending to allocate resources this way largely through headteacher-driven decisions.

In terms of the longer-term school-to-school work (stage two) a number of partnerships were considering the local clustering of schools, sometimes called consortia (such as Wigan, where the partnership was to 'hold these to account'). Some arrangements were very new, and others such as in Richmond had obviously been in place for some time. The clusters varied in nature: some were primarily primary school-based like the learning communities described earlier, and some were cross-phase, though these create the developmental problems I discussed for secondary schools. In some cases, these consortia were also the basis for dividing or allocating LA or ex-LA services, in which case *they themselves* – like academy chains or Teaching School Alliances – become the middle tier.

The point for deep partnerships and hence for longer-term school improvement is that the work is not then primarily about intervention but how these new or established groupings help establish mutual trust, develop their own systems for sharing data and expertise and develop the basis for joint practice development. We cannot tell from these short reports whether or how such developments feature in their respective plans or visions, or how significant they could be – they weren't constructed primarily to do this and perhaps these questions were not specifically asked.

The Southend Education Trust, however, did express the intention to build strong school-to-school relationships; in Brighton and Hove, central funding was provided for local partnerships, apparently largely on the model of Charles's authority. In the report on York, a small authority with a strong common local spatial identity, 'some impressive examples of joint practice development' were given where clusters had been LA-driven but were now 'very much managed by schools' (Crossley, 2013a: 7). And in Wigan, an authority praised by Her Majesty's Chief Inspector (Ofsted, 2012), the LA 'zero-based' the approach, transferring 'responsibilities to a series of school-led clusters', partly in response to the 'funding crisis' and the 'exiting [of the] LA school improvement advisers' (Crossley, 2013b: 3).

But this sort of work – building depth and the means to do it – does not simply evolve from partnership work. It must be envisioned, prioritized, planned and resourced. It takes time, as the comments made by the headteachers I interviewed in the learning communities affirm, and there the LA had initiated the process. Of course, some schools may seek deep partnerships with more distant schools, perhaps with similar data profiles, as was the case in the City Challenges (Hutchings *et al.*, 2012) and the girls' school mentioned, but this again raises the issue of there being too many clubs.

Providing challenge and legitimacy in the school-led system

This deeper and longer-term work – the transition to the second stage of the model – requires more than simply having, as Hatcher says, 'preventive and remedial strategic visions' that position LAs as 'relays of the government's performance agenda' (2014: 365). The studies cited here show clearly that this might well be all that some LAs have been attempting. From the points of view of headteachers this may help LA survival but it will not address the deeper issue of keeping heads challenged, or the 'mountain range' Richard spoke of, or indeed the continuing overall inequity.

As Andrew, the primary outstanding academy head said, far more clearly than I:

> … where we're going now with the … reforms … the thing is how do you provide that 'challenge' in inverted commas … that continuing motor for inspiration, pull, push, whatever you want to call it, that keeps people in our sorts of positions wanting to go and improve what they do for children?

And his secondary counterpart Thomas reflected on the role that governors could play:

> The whole notion of governance and line management and challenge for heads, I think – it's the huge potential problem in the system. You know we seem to be at the moment in a situation where in many schools, heads are … line managed by chairs of governors with very long-term relationships that would be … I would never say cosy [but] … I've known the chair of governors here all the time I've been here but we've never socialized together … any of those kind of things … Equally because of our

relationship she knows everything about the school, you know. I
do tell her everything and therefore she's part of the decision ...

Ofsted (2012: 13) said that schools had attained outstanding status
by, among other things, 'challenging underperformance'. Whatever the
strengths of the new versions of SIPs that heads were seeking out, whom
they might meet four times a year, this is not quite the routine relationship
advocated in the Hargreaves paper about 'mature' partnerships (2012b).
Not to labour this point, what is it that gets heads and schools that have
achieved national benchmarks to go on looking for ways to develop and
improve? Whereas 'preventive and remedial' may be a necessary aspect of
national governance, it is not clear that these deeper levels of relationship
are likely to be sustained by such work alone.

In an introduction to a document on the role of the middle tier
(ADCS, 2012), a past president of the Association recommends that LAs
use their 'moral leadership' (*ibid*: 6) and other resources 'to challenge heads
and governors of all types of schools to explain and improve on their own
performance'. For Peter, the well-placed secondary headteacher who had
asked the LA to 'work with [his school] rather than against' it, such a
challenge would have fallen on deaf ears. In other places, most often from
regret, headteachers were less likely to see the LA playing such a role because
of its lack of capability and not necessarily its legitimacy. But strategically,
if some cannot, then none can. Most important, for challenge to be effective
– that is, listened to, understood and acted on – the right to challenge needs
to be *earned*. It has to have legitimacy *and* authority. Many LAs have now,
sadly, lost this authority.

As part of the preparatory work for this book, I examined
documentation for three developing partnership arrangements with schools
in urban LAs in different parts of the country, in discussion with Julian who
had been involved in some of their development.

All had been driven initially by the LA but had now been taken up by
headteacher groups, sometimes facilitated by Julian. One document produced
at an early stage of a partnership set out a range of 'conceptualizations',
such as 'systematic support' and 'coordination'. Interestingly, the words of
the National College Maturity Model (Hargreaves, 2012b) are used under
nearly every one of the conceptualizations. Saying it is one thing but Julian
was using the drivers identified by Hargreaves to help the heads assess their
own progress, as noted earlier. A 'challenge group' has since been set up in
this LA to take forward such work chaired by a secondary headteacher. This
is in an authority described in one of the review documents cited above,

not named here to preserve anonymity. But none of the heads involved at strategic level in this continuing work was aware of what council officers had been describing for the Pritchard national review.

A 'new architecture' document had been drafted for school improvement in another LA, taken forward by a group of headteachers, with representatives of the National College and the LA. This, too, was LA-wide. It was made up of a wide range of stakeholders, overwhelmingly headteachers (of good or outstanding schools 'with a sustained track record of supporting school improvement outside their own school'), but included two senior LA officers. This new arrangement is intended to address school improvement matters in the LA, and begins to describe protocols whereby individual school developments can be discussed confidentially. It sets out ambitions for collective moral responsibility, sharing and analysing data, developing system capacity and evaluating improvement work. There is a separate group with more open invite meetings for supporting school-to-school partnerships where this deeper work could be discussed or progressed. The architecture could provide a framework for it.

Finally, a metropolitan authority in the South East undertook a strategic review of its school improvement function early in the Coalition Government, formally reporting in 2012. This was akin to the Hertfordshire reorganization of its own school improvement service, so was not as radical or wide-ranging as some of the other partnership arrangements I have described. Although it was agreed to take the least cost option, I mention it here because the level and nature of headteacher involvement in the project changed over the lifetime of the project. From heads being fairly deeply involved in the discussions and consultations in the early stages of the project – in common with good practice in many LAs – it moved to a situation where headteachers became reluctant to volunteer to join appointment panels for LA staff.

LA legitimacy: Professional, community and elected

The right to challenge practice and outcomes in schools, which as we have seen has to be earned, can be legitimized in different ways. The professional right, based on similar experience, understanding of the work context and trust, is at the heart of the successful peer-to-peer learning in the school networks Hargreaves described.

Community-based authority is the approach being considered by Thomas in thinking about his relationship with his chair of governors. This relationship also needs to be based on trust: both Thomas and his chair are motivated by what the school helps its students to achieve. For the chair this is rooted in years of living in the community and giving oversight to its school. Parents have a similar locally focused authority, based on their ceding their children to the school for 14 per cent of their lives together with the major responsibility of shaping the next stages of their trajectories.

Democratic authority, however, needs to be rooted not in experience or understanding but instead in an individual, or groups of individuals, elected to carry out a political programme in a community or communities. They might be united by a well-defined sense of place and mission, as in Birmingham, Manchester or Bristol, or by a vague sense of belonging among people who will never meet – I suspect that geographically large counties such as Wiltshire or Somerset fall into this category – or by being an artificial grouping of communities forced together a generation ago by local government reorganization and given an artificial name that inspires little loyalty or recognition. I suspect that many boroughs and unitary authorities fall into this latter category.

The moral authority in local government that comes with being elected or appointed by elected politicians is in serious decline in the English education polity and may well be irrecoverable. Some of the most telling aspects of Hatcher's analysis of the emerging LA-wide partnerships are reflected in his account of how system leaders in Birmingham secondary schools 'preferred to rely on direct relations between heads without any involvement of the LA' (Hatcher, 2014: 360) and how a council proposal for a city-wide partnership eventually became a 'partnership led and controlled by headteachers and funded by subscription' (*ibid*: 361). Tellingly, he says the council handed over the writing of parts of the city's 'strategic vision' to headteachers as in Hertfordshire, Brighton and Hove, Liverpool, and York. Crossley (2013a: 7) expresses this move in York LA as 'letting go'. The issue for Birmingham, according to Hatcher, is that headteachers were not willing to have a vision imposed on them by the council and involving the Chamber of Commerce with its interest in employability.

In cities such as Leicester (LGA/SOLACE, 2013: 12–13) a 'strategic overview' of raising achievement is represented as a flow chart, from the *City Mayor's Delivery Plan* down to work in, and with, schools. But it remains to be seen whether such council conceptions will survive or have any meaning. All the officers I interviewed spoke about aspects of 'letting go' that varied from staying neutral while schools made their own strategic choices, to the council 'doing itself out of business' by setting up the learning communities.

Education may now be transitioning towards a professional democracy locally, but it is not democratic in the sense of a wider community having an input into a key public service. Arrangements are being made through school-to-school partnerships that let schools make the decisions about what might formerly have been termed the 'strategic direction of the service', either in a local geographical location or across an entire LA area. But as Hatcher points out, 'schools' actually means 'headteachers', and each of the new RSCs are also supported by, and are responsible to, boards of elected outstanding headteachers.

I return to the consequences of this in the final chapter. Hatcher calls the redeployment of responsibility 'depoliticisation' (2014: 368), that is, education no longer features in local political objectives. Most aspects of schools are removed from the purview of the local state. Headteachers' complaints about LA functioning, including about elected members, are not new – I have 22 years' experience of such complaints – but my interviews indicated that there has been a fundamental shift in headteacher perceptions and attitudes.

Richard, the head quoted at the top of this chapter, spoke of the 'hollowing out [of the] 'middle of' the LA, to leave a large 'senior layer' with very high salaries and 'strange job titles', namely the strategic directors in his authority. His 'middle' referred to those senior staff, discussed earlier, with experience of senior management in schools and on whose professional and moral authority trust – and loyalty – were founded.

The head of the girls' school in the South East worked in an LA that no longer called headteacher meetings. Officers asked to attend heads' meetings when they had an item they wished to discuss. She reported the recent attendance at such a meeting of 'an interim head of achievement' but said the only thing the heads were thinking at the time was 'how long [is this person] going to be here?'. I have heard similar comments elsewhere. Douglas, the senior adviser, recalled that he and his adviser colleagues were trying to remember when the last directors' meeting had been; it had been nearly a year ago and these meetings have since ceased.

In some areas, therefore, LAs are also moving out from the discursive influence of heads and their schools where they can air strategic directions and developments, just as schools are drifting further away from LAs. I have been struck by the willingness on the part of all interviewees to talk about these issues, and as said often, have the impression that they do not have the opportunity to do so elsewhere.

I asked heads about the role of elected members and whether they had any presence in schools, perhaps as governors. One made a number of comments about the 'quality' of elected members in his unitary authority. A head in the metropolitan area said that 'when you get beyond the few key people' who are senior members of the council, the 'quality' was 'very poor'.

But then satisfying secondary heads has never been a criterion for achieving democratic office! Some heads, especially at secondary level, had governors who are politicians, while others had experience of planning and traffic decisions and the like that seemed to them to be entirely motivated by party politics. Though these comments were unfavourable, some heads still wanted some elected body to have oversight of their area, or 'place', as Andrew did. Others just did not see the need.

There are wider arguments to make about this apparent transition from elected to professional democracy. Mark, who had worked with free schools, challenged the very notion of 'democratic'. He felt that the new free schools were 'giving accountability to people in a different sort of way, because ... they are created with the support of local parents and they're very much reliant on ... parents choosing to send their children to them. [They have] a kind of very close relationship with the school'. This represents the community model of authority.

On being pressed further about the traditional operation of a public LA meeting, with public galleries possibly full of people – many of them probably parents – who disagreed with a decision about to be made, Mark thought they were possibly, though not necessarily, unrepresentative of a wider public. The processes involved could not guarantee representativeness either way.

Such a mobilization model has been utilized for some years by campaigning organizations as part of local democracy, such as the Anti Academies Alliance, to try to resist the 'forced' academization of schools identified as RI or worse. The great force of the campaigning parents' and teachers' argument about compulsory status change is that it has sometimes been proposed *against the wishes of all the local people*. Here again is the community model of authority, and the simple governing body vote necessary for post-2010 converter academies, allegedly sometimes taken over the summer holiday, is quite different from earlier conversions to grant-maintained or foundation status as it has been since 1999. Here two votes were required, plus consultation with parents and often a public meeting where parents had an opportunity to hear from both sides.

The community authority argument is that significant change should not be effected without the *agreement* of those directly involved – a hard criterion to meet as even minor decisions such as changes in catchment areas can be hotly contested, as Matthew agreed. There are other issues for LAs, though.

Catherine's quote at the top of this chapter restates the powerful case for the LA as the only democratically constituted body in an area and, leaving aside what has been explored here about the mechanism to support school improvement, the only one legitimately able, therefore, to develop a local vision for all communities. Leaving aside low electoral turnout, however, the daily workings of LAs (particularly on major decisions – school reorganization plans, closures, planning new places and so on) can be criticized since the replacement by cabinet government, with responsible individual elected executive members, of the Committees that had been around for nearly a hundred years previously. A large, deliberative and visible committee meeting, where votes are taken on a major decision by elected representatives, receiving advice from senior officers set out in reports sent out in advance, with members of the public in the gallery watching, is quite different from the cabinet member publicly announcing his or her decision at a regular calendared and announced meeting.

With the advent of directly elected mayors, procedures have changed again. In one of the urban authorities in which Julian was working, the elected mayor had retained all executive power for himself so even cabinet meetings were not deliberative, leaving cabinet and full council to *advise* on nearly all matters except the budget and individual planning decisions, with the occasional other weighty matter referred there. I checked this information on the council's website. At one of the LAs where I interviewed, the mayor was of a different political party from the cabinet and reportedly did not speak at all at cabinet meetings, yet still had executive power. An argument can be made for cabinet and mayoral government, but not on the grounds of operating an open, deliberative democracy.

One of the mechanisms for holding executive members and local government – and other – local services to account is through so-called scrutiny commissions. The Children's Services Commission in another LA had taken expert evidence on the future role of the LA in relation to schools and published a lengthy report setting out its aspirations. This document shows little apparent input from schools, though some of the elected members were governors. Headteachers were reportedly ignorant of the document and, as in Birmingham, did not wish to be told what their role was by the LA. This again is the classic 'legitimation crisis' (Cooke and Muir, 2012) for the LA, though not for the first time in the past 25 years. This was echoed in some form in all the LA areas I visited and, possibly, most of those described in the section on school partnerships. Even the Local Government Association (2013) recognizes there is a crisis in democracy in England.

Chapter 7

Equity and the developing English education polity

To complain of the age we live in, to murmur at the present possessors of power, to lament the past, to conceive extravagant hopes of the future, are the common dispositions of the greatest part of mankind; indeed the necessary effects of the ignorance and levity of the vulgar. Such complaints and humours have existed in all times; yet as all times have not been alike, true political sagacity manifests itself, in distinguishing that complaint which only characterizes human nature, from those which are the symptoms of the particular distemperature of our own air and season.

Nobody, I believe, will consider it merely as the language of spleen or disappointment, if I say, that there is something particularly alarming in the present conjuncture.

(Edmund Burke, 1770: 4)

The next 5 years will be about going further, in particular, not accepting any failure in the system – however difficult that may be. One, we need zero tolerance of the failing schools that still exist within the system. One of the great frustrations of the past 5 years was that because of bureaucratic rules, we could only intervene in 50% of the schools rated 'inadequate' by Ofsted. So as part of our Education Bill, we will sweep away these rules and make sure every 'inadequate' school will be turned into an academy, with new leadership. Next we need to improve what I have called 'coasting schools'. Today the Education Secretary will set out to Parliament the principles we will apply to judge whether schools are coasting. Coasting schools are those where standards have been mediocre for too many years and aren't improving quickly enough. Schools where standards could and should be higher, given their intake and potential. These include some schools rated 'Requires Improvement' – but who aren't improving quickly enough. And other schools rated 'Good' at their last inspection – but which haven't been maintaining high standards since. They are giving children 'just enough' to avoid falling beneath our floor standards.

But frankly 'just enough' isn't good enough for my children, and it shouldn't be for yours. So we're going to say to those schools: if you're not making fast enough progress in raising standards, you have to change and if you can't do it yourself, you have to become a sponsored Academy and welcome in people with a proven track record of running outstanding schools. Taken together, these changes mean we will turn around 1,000 more failing schools and improve hundreds more coasting schools. This will all be incredibly difficult to push through. But I see it as a fundamental test of this government to see these reforms through.

(David Cameron, 2015)

Looking forward: The developing polity for schools
The regional education state

Burke's lament of 'complaints and humours' could be applied to the briefing issued to the associates network of the ADCS on the publication of the new Education and Adoption Bill by the Conservative Government (ADCS, 2015). The author of this briefing referred to the RSCs who are to be given new intervention powers in the bill as: 'Satraps for the Secretary of State, that is, civil servants directly accountable to the Secretary of State with delegated authority' (*ibid*: 2).

This signals a significant and continuing reconfiguring of the national and local states, not unnaturally resented by these senior LA officers. One of the RSCs I interviewed just before he took up post in 2014 described the reception he had received at a recent regional LA officers' meeting as already 'hostile, very hostile'.

The regional arm of the national state in England is developing rapidly. It is moving on from being an efficient way of overseeing the increasing numbers of academies and free schools. Presently, RSCs recruit and vet new academy sponsors, make recommendations on new free school and academy proposals to the Secretary of State and mobilize system leadership resources for academies and free schools at risk – NLEs, LLEs, NSSs, SLEs and Teaching School Alliances. They take advice from, and involve, their headteacher advisory boards (HTBs) as they do so. But RSCs have access to maintained schools' data too, and they were inducted after their appointment into the national arrangements for intervention into *all* schools determined by the minister. This future RSC made it clear that there would be 'no hanging about' now for schools that require improvement, even if they were maintained.

The new legislation brings further powers to RSCs for a hard status academy conversion if a softer intervention with a maintained school – working with the LA and mobilizing system leadership resources – has not succeeded over a short period of time. A speedier conversion process will be possible once shorter periods are allowed for objections and – by implication – campaigns such as those Alan described. The expectation now is that conversion will follow automatically after an 'inadequate' judgement, some RIs and even some 'Good' ones, depending on progress. This is a command-and-control process.

Ofsted

Ofsted has been regionalized too, though not entirely matching the boundaries of the RSCs. It has its own regional directors.

The management of school inspection has been brought in house for schools, with effect from 1 September 2015. Instead of employing additional inspectors (AIs) contracted by three national Inspection Service Providers (Tribal, SERCO and CfBT), inspections will now be undertaken by the newly named 'Ofsted inspectors', the 'vast majority of [whom] are serving practitioners' and who 'will be contracted with directly' by Ofsted (Ofsted, 2015b: 10). These Ofsted inspectors have been through a selection process with several stages; a number of the AIs I interviewed had not made it through. At the time of writing, Ofsted had announced a 'purge [of] more than 1,200 inspectors', according to Vaughan (2015), some of whom failed due to a lack of 'skill in writing reports' (*ibid*: 6). Some AIs I interviewed, and Julian and Jean also confirmed this informally. Each member of Her Majesty's Inspectorate – also based regionally – now has a group of 10–20 inspectors for whom they will effectively be line managers.

This may not affect the number of inspections undertaken, except inasmuch as the new inspection framework will have new requirements (Ofsted, 2015b), but may increase the proportional involvement of system leaders. Outstanding headteachers I interviewed who were lead inspectors, however, limit the number of inspections they do each year because of the potential impact on their own schools. Jean, who was working for one of the former Inspection Service Providers, said in 2014 that of the hundreds of AIs they had as associates, many no longer volunteered for inspection anyway because of its more demanding requirements and strict deadlines. Headteacher inspectors tended to write their reports at weekends.

National expectations

The ratcheting up of school standards has been implemented by politician-driven rising floor standards, on the one hand (the non-achievement of which itself has constituted grounds for intervention since 2002), and the changing requirements of what is acceptable in each of the inspection grades, on the other.

The floor targets at secondary level now stand at 60 per cent of students achieving '5 good GCSEs' together with an above-average proportion of pupils making acceptable progress. For primary schools, the respective figures are 85 per cent achieving what is now regarded as an 'acceptable secondary-ready standard in reading, writing and maths' over three years, taking into account the revised forms of assessment for 11-year-olds.

The most significant change in inspection has been the replacement, since September 2012, of the old 'Satisfactory' grade for an Ofsted inspection by RI. This has been accompanied by the other rising expectations, especially to achieve 'Good' and 'Outstanding'.

And schools are expected to do better for *all* their children. Since 2013 there has been additional emphasis on the difference in attainment outcomes for disadvantaged children and their peers. In 2014 at least one Ofsted regional director wrote to all heads of schools where the gap in pupils' attainment exceeded 20 percentage points, drawing their attention to the issue. One secondary headteacher I interviewed – of an outstanding school – confirmed the receipt of such a letter.

Although Ofsted examines how school governance arrangements affect pupil outcomes and progress, there is an increasing emphasis on leadership, itself not new (Gunter, 2012) but now morally driven. Her Majesty's Chief Inspector says:

> Great leadership is at the heart of the three major reforms Ofsted is making to inspection from September, 2015. Using the new common inspection framework, inspectors will look at leaders' vision and ambition for all children and learners. They will want to see how leaders set the culture of their school or provider and how they ensure that all learners – particularly the most disadvantaged – make strong progress from their different starting points.
>
> (Ofsted, 2015b: 2)

How to think about the model of academy status in 2015
What model?

With a primary emphasis on leadership rather than governance and all school interventions now potentially focused on academy conversion, the academy model itself – preferred by the Government (Conservative Party, 2015) – has additional significance and must be examined. This is especially so in the light of the prime ministerial target for the conversion of 1,000 failing schools and 'several hundred' others, with renewed attention given to coasting schools.

There is no single academy model of success. Connelly *et al.* summarize attainment and equity gaps in their review of earlier research studies of academies as follows:

> There is mixed evidence on academies. It is important to note that the available evaluations of Academy schools relate to those schools which were struggling before being converted

into Academies. Many of the new academies were already being successful before conversion, and there is no evidence to suggest that these schools are more successful than schools with comparable intakes. Academies do not appear to have been successful in reducing SES [socio-economic status] segregation between schools.

(Connelly *et al.*, 2014: 34)

Connelly *et al.* add that 'there is not currently any clear evidence available of the effectiveness of free schools' (*ibid*: 34).

When the House of Commons Education Committee (2015) considered attainment as part of its report on academies and free schools, it similarly found the evidence complex. Even before 2010, academies were reporting mixed success, it said, but this was against a background where 'however measured, the overall state of [all] schools [was also] … improv[ing] during the course of the academisation programme' (*ibid*: 23). That is, all schools' results were going up.

But no straightforward evidence *could* be expected or guaranteed. The Coalition's Academies Act 2010 reoriented the academy policy. The original conception of academies was as an intervention into 'struggling schools' (Connelly *et al.*, 2014) and, in the very early days, the change in status was accompanied by large injections of capital. But this was succeeded in 2010 by the converter model, which was taken advantage of by schools already considered successful, for many of which no major changes were made. Converters now vastly outnumber forced conversions, as Alan noted.

So there are at least two academy models, and more when taking into account the governance differences between free-standing academies and those in chains, and more still when the differences between chains are considered. The point of the Connelly *et al.* and House of Commons considerations is that success is uneven and depends on what conversion allows to happen within the school.

Academy conversion in the post-2015 polity

From 2015, academy status is an intervention for schools shaped by a more widely cast net of Ofsted and data outcomes and, at the same time, a predominantly pragmatic matter for headteachers of successful maintained schools, especially if they wish to develop a wider system role themselves or develop more systematic working relationships with their neighbours.

There remain good reasons for opposing academy status. The streamlined approval process will allow less time for any local campaign to work. Depending on how the governing body changes, some new schools may not have the community legitimacy that campaigners and others including myself consider important for the children. But in schools like Peter's, after over thirty years of the social realities of parental choice, a school-places market and school stratification (Riddell, 2003), it is difficult to define precisely what the community is, beyond the parents who of course change.

There is little democratic oversight of these schools any more, but in any case there are problems with the democratic legitimacy of LAs. Further, because of LAs' declining professional capacity and powers, it will become increasingly difficult for any single body to see it as its role to take an overall view of state education in a community, city or county. This responsibility has now shifted to the regional state. Some of the new academies will have single school sponsors in another LA area or be members of chains managed from a head office more distant than the local council HQ.

One risk with a chain managed from a distance that has just taken over an at-risk school – perhaps asked to do so by the RSC – is that it will see 'getting the school right' as more important than engaging the local community. Julian described conversion as being seen by some chains as a sort of technical or technicist exercise: the chain brings its own brand of secondary education to another local branch. It is surely important that the community and parents feature somewhere in this change, even when the community is hard to identify in some schools serving urban areas.

The system overall is increasingly being run by headteachers, but that does not guarantee increased autonomy. In some of the chains, depending generally on the outcome status of the schools, the management arrangements can be described as providing only limited or even prescribed autonomy. Chain management teams top-slice aspects of school budgets and move staff from school to school as employees of the one organization, albeit for the positive purpose of enabling joint professional development. Interim leadership is imposed and performance in schools managed from outside. Most LAs have not acted like this for years!

I argue here that limited or prescribed autonomy is an important part of the developing two-stage model post-2015 for schools and the teaching profession. In any case, although McKinsey (2007; 2010) argued that increased school autonomy was considered the necessary accompaniment to a high-performing system, the House of Commons Education Committee (2015) observed what a 'complex relationship [there was between] attainment, autonomy, collaboration and accountability' (*ibid*: 3).

Chains, other middle-tier bodies and none at all

If academy conversion cannot guarantee the future success of at-risk schools, the performance of academy chains is also variable. Both Julian and Jean were of the view that some chains have virtually no capacity for school support or intervention. In some, there is 'nothing there at all' at HQ (Julian). At the time of writing, Ofsted had just issued a letter to a multi-academy trust after a 'focused inspection' – where a large number of schools are all inspected together – saying:

> The Trust's academies have a variable record of improvement. While some have improved or sustained effective performance, too many academies have not improved quickly enough. A legacy of weak challenge and insufficiently systematic improvement work has resulted in slow progress in nearly half the academies.

In addition, the report states that 'some groups of pupils do not achieve well', including 'disadvantaged pupils, particularly boys', when compared to their peers nationally. The identity of this well-known chain – not one I visited – is immaterial, but it could not be conceived as an improved alternative governance mechanism to LAs. Its offices are nowhere near some of its schools.

So the variability of LAs has been replaced in some places by the variability of academy chains that are nationally accountable to the Secretary of State by means of Ofsted and the RSCs. Hutchings *et al.* (2014) point out, moreover, that the performance of chains is variable with respect to disadvantaged children, as the Ofsted letter shows.

I touched on the role of churches when I described my interviews with the heads of faith schools who were considering what they would do next about academy conversion within the context of the developing polity. The Church of England's work on this is well advanced. In a publication considering the future of diocesan boards, the 'ten marks of a high-performing Diocesan Board of Education' are said to include the fact that:

> The [diocesan] Education Team uses data effectively to analyse the performance of all diocesan schools, identify schools that need support and enable the brokering of support to ensure school effectiveness.
>
> (Church of England, 2013: 3)

This is familiar language and does not relate only to voluntary aided schools; the diocese will thus become another form of middle tier. I have not gathered direct data about the work of the Church, but the dioceses local to my home have expanded their teams and, as Alison said, her school was examining the possibility of an arrangement for academy status with the diocesan MAT.

But the really important point here is that a very large proportion of academies are 'free-standing and not part of any formal grouping' (Simkins, 2015: 6). Simkins discusses the 'potential for fragmentation with a diversity of governance emerging as a key feature of the new schooling landscape' (2014:1) and says that in the three LAs where he was gathering data, 45 per cent of the schools fell into this category, the vast majority of which were converters. Secondary heads of converters I interviewed had a variety of partnership arrangements, but among them I could not identify a single significant well-established one based on trust. Remember Julian's comment about the 'Billy no-mates' heads, uncertain of the future, for whom the developing LA-wide partnership arrangements could be seen as providing a home or different form of middle tier.

So what has emerged for academy status in 2015 is not one simple picture, regardless of how conversion is accelerated over the next few years. Alison and other primary heads may not see 'academy' as being the preferred status – Arthur's school is still a maintained school – but it is already seen as such at secondary level. Some 24 per cent of secondary schools are in a MAT, 31 per cent of schools are academies not in a MAT and 5 per cent are free schools, university technical colleges and studio schools, leaving 40 per cent maintained (NFER, 2015). By contrast, 87 per cent of primary schools were still maintained in 2014, but we know this will change.

Understanding what it all means

Academy status as intervention, now to be initiated after casting the net much wider, needs to be understood as the means by which RSCs take over the responsibility for school improvement plans – nothing less and nothing more, despite the political rhetoric. Reducing LA roles, this represents a structural change that ushers in a new system. The assemblage shifts again.

Will it work? The two future RSCs I interviewed were impressive. Both could describe in practical and straightforward terms what they were already doing in their roles at the time to help improve schools under their supervision or associateship. It was easy to see how this could be extended to wider groups of schools. RSCs also have the support and time of a group of outstanding headteachers on their advisory boards, one of whom I interviewed (Dominic). The practical language of these emerging players reflects that of Daniel and some of the heads I interviewed about the five or ten steps necessary to 'get to good' or outstanding.

Although I believe these two RSCs have the capacity to supervise an expanded number of improvement plans, their success and that of their colleagues will depend on the quality and extent of the system leadership resources that can be mobilized from NLEs, LLEs, SLEs, NSSs and TSAs and new sponsors. I have no data on TSAs except indirectly from the heads associated with them, reflected in some of the previous comments. Some reviews have been undertaken of their work and development, however, for example with respect to their relationships with universities (Greany and Brown, 2015) and more generally of their work (Stoll, 2015). I suspect these could provide additional lessons for partnership working more broadly.

Nationally, therefore, the development of an effective network of TSAs (DfE, 2010a), as well as the recruitment of extra sponsor schools and national and local leaders, need to remain a priority. The capacity of such a network needs to be kept under review. One example of good practice I learned about in a city in the South West was that the teaching school had amalgamated its CPD programme with that previously provided by the LA and it was housed in one of the city's universities. This represents capacity-building.

A potentially more reliable and consistent system is emerging than that provided through LAs, but it is still in development. As noted, the House of Commons Education Committee was taking evidence during 2015 on the roles of RSCs (see http://tinyurl.com/pane6te) and the issue of inconsistency was raised at the first of its open sessions.

New roles for LAs

Meanwhile, LAs will also be in transition in terms of their school improvement roles. For some with little capacity that do not know their schools, this will represent hardly any change. But those LAs that have kept large school improvement teams – sometimes in separate organizations – are more likely to be affected, albeit in different ways and at a different pace. In at least the transition, LAs may continue aspects of their risk-identification role, and where they are still in touch with schools and have respected staff with recognized moral authority – bought in or otherwise – could continue to help RSCs with building system capacity by suggesting people apply, making recommendations and so forth. But it is likely that their brokering and signposting role may fall away more quickly and they will not commission work in the future for at-risk schools, broadly in line with the Academies Commission recommendations (2013).

None of this is particularly welcomed by this ex-LA officer but the reality of developments in place before 2015 and those continuing after needs to be grasped pragmatically and positively by all, without 'lamenting the past, or conceiving extravagant hopes for the future', as Burke put it. This leaves the two newer roles I would recommend LAs consider.

The first is in relation to helping develop long-term sustainable school-to-school partnerships based on trust, sharing data and jointly developing practice to improve what they offer to all children. These local networks are vital for moving beyond the risk assessment/deploying system leadership resources role as we increasingly look as a society to networks – bazaars – rather than cathedrals. The latter cannot carry forward development beyond whatever is deemed acceptable nationally, and they are not necessarily trusted or well regarded. Networks need to be nurtured on a very local level, taking into account the different professional relationships required by primary and secondary schools. This will probably mean acting much more locally than the LA-wide partnerships described, with their varying roles, though some are engaged in this work.

But the vision for these partnerships has to be developed by headteachers, as they are now in the driving seat of the polity, and are the ones resourced. They require committed and authoritative people who are outside the national accountability mechanisms to work with them. And the heads will all need to know each other better. Those LAs with system knowledge and experienced and committed staff could facilitate this process. The LA-wide partnerships that do exist could help with this work by bringing people together, drawing on collective system resources and visioning in the area they serve. It may be easier to do this in places that have a strong spatial identity, such as cities and towns, where people can share their moral commitment to the area and meet up in the pursuit of making it better.

The second potential new role may not be so new for some LAs. It relates to vision and the earlier comments about change management from a distance, constructions of technicist solutions for school improvement and the lack of importance attached to *place* reported by many of the people I interviewed, including Julian and Charles. Academy status should not mean isolation from community: Thomas's comments attest to this, and Dominic spoke of the need for enrichment programmes in the particular communities his chain's first secondary school served.

So links with the community can be made and prioritized by schools, even if the community dimension of governing bodies disappears in some places, along with all their other responsibilities. The voices of parents and students need to be heard. As Adrian, the chief officer quoted in Chapter 6, said, parents need redress for grievance but this can seem remote in the new system and often inaccessible. The LA could clearly have a continuing championing role in this regard.

But LAs could also have a more developed and positive role, especially in deprived communities. Young people spend a relatively small part of their time in schooling and education. Most of their mental constructs and frames for interpretation and reinterpretation of learning are formed in continuous relation to their home and community experiences. This, as Kerr *et al.* (2014) aver, affects how *place* is conceived and carried over into school. It circumscribes performance outcomes, generally worse in deprived communities, and constrains ways of improving them with the concomitant implications for social, educational, occupational and – properly – wellbeing trajectories. We know that the nature of the school attended can make up to 22 per cent difference in outcomes at the age of 16, so it is vital to prioritize processes to maximize educational possibilities for disadvantaged students.

Kerr *et al.* review the potential of area-based initiatives with their previous mixed success (Power *et al.*, 2005). They advocate 'children's communities' or 'zones' that can 'operate across childhood and adolescent years, and across all aspects of children's lives'. Such an approach is 'an acknowledgement of the interconnectedness of outcomes and of the processes producing outcomes that we have identified' (Kerr *et al.*, 2014: 194). Children's communities are focused on areas and communities of disadvantage but certain communities are formed by the wider political economy, or 'ecology', as Kerr *et al.* acknowledge. Specifically, they can concentrate on a range of outcomes for children, not just in learning but also those that affect it, such as health.

On a broader front, such communities have the capability to develop community-set priorities within a wider geographical context – avoiding the 'ghettoization' of earlier regeneration initiatives. This approach allows for the wider involvement in learning that Fielding and Moss argue for: ways of extending classrooms into the community – and back again into school – that I have also advocated (Riddell, 2003). A children's community can incorporate aspects of the extended schools provision reviewed enthusiastically by Cummings *et al.* (2011).

The communities reviewed by Kerr *et al.* have been run by different organizations, including charities and academy trusts, with LA involvement in all cases. It appears that LAs can be well placed, bringing a variety of their own services to bear, to take a slightly wider view of the place the unit of community covers, whether this is a major urban area of social housing and deprivation or a few isolated troubled streets in a sparsely populated rural area. LAs should arguably see this as a fundamental part of their democratic role, not least as being *champions* for vulnerable children (as Catherine said) and looking beyond access agreements. Many LAs have area-based or partnership mechanisms that could decide how to address and contribute to this and prioritize and encourage such communities to develop their visions. This could provide a new balance between democratic and professional roles and help establish authority where this has disappeared.

Funding and capacity are issues here too. This is not going to come from LAs except on a pump-priming basis – as we have seen from school-to-school support – unless national funding settlements change. So it has to come from the charitable sector or the wider mechanisms of philanthrocapitalism discussed earlier, uncomfortable as this may seem. Money from such sources is already finding its way into such projects, sometimes in the form of facilitating staff development in transnational companies through pupil mentoring and sponsorship (Riddell, 2013). This further redefines notions of democratic oversight, but there is potential here for new notions of LA ring-holding: some of them are on to this already. The LGA (2014a) assumes the local visioning work is core to the LA's purposes. Pupil premium funding could possibly be used for part of the work – driven by schools – without losing its focus on the disadvantaged.

The final issue here *is* the role of professionals – LA or other – in such initiatives. Parachuting professionals into deprived communities raises an old debate around regeneration initiatives. It needs thought, even when the professionals manage the local delivery of services or when the work needs to follow the priorities of a charity decided elsewhere and properly accountable to extremely distant trustees. A senior official in the Department for Communities and Local Government I interviewed in 2005, in connection with Local Area Agreements, articulated the role of these professionals as being to help local people address 'some of their immediate concerns very early', but then helping them 'quickly … to raise their sights [and] think about the role of their neighbourhood in the borough, city or even sub-region … and connect in with the institutions that operate at those levels'. He saw this as being about long-term sustainability and ensuring that a 'particular neighbourhood [does not remain] the armpit neighbourhood of the city'. There remains important work here for LAs, schools and others. All should seize it in the interest of equity.

Conclusion: Motors and models for change

The shifting assemblage of the English schools polity is transforming yet again in the first year of the Conservative Government. There is the potential for fragmentation in the landscape of schooling identified by Simkins (2015) and Simkins *et al.* (2014). Even the relatively well-positioned heads in terms of their Ofsted judgements and outcome data (Coldron *et al.*, 2014) whom I interviewed feel the insecurity caused by both the uncertain relationships and their own position. Clustering and partnering arrangements vary widely by phase and purpose. LAs are, or will be, moving away from more traditional but varying orientations towards their school improvement responsibilities. As the old roles fall away they should consider new ones based on helping build the deep partnerships I have written about here and their developed championing and visioning role, especially in deprived communities.

Meanwhile, the regional state develops, taking on new powers with a Conservative Government that it will exercise under stringent national expectations. This is developing into a tough, more uniform interventionist national policy lever for the small number of schools not achieving such expectations. This command-and-control mechanism represents the 'directing state' at work (Lodge and Hood, 2012) – hardly a market mechanism. This is not inconsistent, however, with other analyses of the neoliberal state such as that of Crouch (2011).

Given the likely consistency of the regional state compared with what is left of the old system for maintained schools that it is replacing, it will most likely lead to dramatic change, especially in schools falling below national benchmarks. This will depend on the further expansion of the system leadership infrastructure. Risk-assessed intervention represents the first stage of the realization of a schools-led system where schools have reached a minimum ('Good') expectation. The interventions will raise outcomes for all children, including the disadvantaged, as this becomes and remains a greater priority. They will thus help achieve greater equity and contribute towards delivering much of the 22 per cent positive effect on learning, a task that is unlikely ever to be complete.

The second stage of realizing the school-led system, building the deep partnerships, is already under way, as much of the evidence presented in Chapter 5 in particular shows. As yet it is incomplete and variable, and the work for it can also never, by definition, be finished. The RSCs will contribute to stage two through the system leadership structures they build, aided or not by LAs, and the relationships they develop across their regions with their HTBs. Headteachers and heads of academy chains are now taking up the leadership reins for the new self-improving system, as they need to. More must follow. Such processes are tangible right now.

There will always be the need for some intervention – some schools have much more serious mountain ranges to climb than Richard's – and school trajectories are never even. So this will continue even when the 1,000-plus school mountain range signalled by the Prime Minister has been climbed. But less will be required of the RSCs as networks take greater control.

This two-stage model for the schools polity – moving towards many more professional relationships and networks based on trust – has its counterpart in the teaching profession. Long-term security and trust for heads and schools must be underpinned by trust in teachers – which has long been needed in England. There are signs that a new professional model is emerging that may make this possible.

There is a stage one for teachers too. This is about 'getting to good' through consistent and challenging teaching – making possible the minimum progress required for all pupils in their classrooms. Even here we seem to be moving away from the cathedral model of knowledge. Ofsted no longer grades individual lessons or the quality of individuals' teaching, as the 2014 framework for inspection made clear (Ofsted, 2014a). Nor is Ofsted seeking any particular form of lesson or learning interaction.

Progress is what counts. As an inspector I interviewed explained, this is to avoid the 'pyrotechnics phenomenon' whereby inspectors witness an exciting one-off lesson, or part of it, that did not achieve any longer-term learning or progress for the children. As a continuing sign of the times, information indicating that Ofsted was going to focus on progression produced a flurry of new marking policies and practice in schools. So Ofsted issued a new clarification (2015c) to say it was not looking for any specific type or frequency of marking in schools either. There is some way to go on trust – and feeling trusted – still. But this is a significant step.

Daniel made similar comments about the performance management of teachers in his chain. The chain management team observed all the teachers, but this too was about engagement with the children and, most importantly, the progress they were making. They would always 'look at the books for this', not just to see what the marking was like.

Andrew, the head of an outstanding primary academy, reflecting on his own school's improvement journey, spoke about the need to seek a balance between:

... accountability and the level of responsibility that you take, [while] still giving staff the opportunity to breathe – professionally breathe – and ... really focus on the practice; they are practitioners, they are constantly looking at stretching and developing ... [developing] that confidence in them to say, 'it didn't quite work, so I'll try this'.

Andrew was absolutely clear that to get to this point his school and teachers had, however, 'delivered the data' and the Ofsted outcome. They had achieved the benchmark. This comment sketches the possible nature of an evolving new and flexible trust, albeit set within a minimum outcome accountability framework of some sort that should be in place for all public services.

Teachers can recognize that they are expected to achieve benchmarks and, once achieved, be given professional discretion and responsibility for how to surpass them and address inequities more deeply. Andrew was not the only head to speak like this; Peter was another and there were many others. This is stage two for the teaching profession. It is a more effective basis for tackling the 22 per cent and engaging – especially in deprived areas – with area initiatives such as children's communities that could begin to tackle inequity more effectively beyond that percentage, developing local complementary social and economic policies.

Much cultural baggage – in many places – has to be cleared away before this can happen generally, but again it is not helped by the continuing shrillness of government announcements. But at some point the transition must be made everywhere from interventions identified on the basis of risk, however helpful they prove, at stage one, to interventions that aid the transition to trust and the longer-term relationships within the profession I have described – stage two – together with those with the communities schools serve. Much rests for the next few years on the shoulders of the RSCs, with their advisory boards, teams and system resources. We should all wish them well in their task.

References

Academies Commission (2013) *Unleashing Greatness: Getting the best from an academised system.* London: RSA. Online. www.rsa.org.uk (accessed 26 November 2014).

ADCS (2012) *The Missing Link: The evolving role of the local authority in school improvement.* London: ADCS.

— (2015) *The Education and Adoption Bill: Updated to include reference to the Queen's speech and the published bill.* London: ADCS.

Anti Academies Alliance (2015) 'Show us the evidence!' Online. http://antiacademies.org.uk/2015/05/show-us-the-evidence (accessed 22 October 2015).

Apple, M. (2012) *Education and Power.* New York: Routledge.

Apple, M. and Beane, J. (2007) *Democratic Schools: Lessons in powerful education.* 2nd ed. Portsmouth, NH: Heinemann.

ASCL (2014) 'Ideas take flight: How the future may look'. *Leader,* 81 (October), 15–17.

Aston, H., Easton, C., Sims, D., Smith, R., Walker, F., Crossley, D., and Crossley-Holland, J. (2013) *What works in enabling school improvement; The role of the middle tier.* Slough: NFER. Online. www.nfer.ac.uk/publications/MTSL02/MTSL02.pdf (accessed 14 July 2014).

Baars, S., Bernardes, E., Elwick, A., Malortie, A., McAleavy, T., McInerney, L., Menzies, L., and Riggall, A. (2014) *Lessons from London Schools: Investigating the success.* London: Centre for British Teachers.

Ball, S. (1990) *Politics and Policy Making in Education: Explorations in policy sociology.* London: Routledge.

— (1994) *Education Reform: A critical and post-structural approach.* Buckingham: Open University Press.

— (1997) 'Policy sociology and critical social research: A personal review of recent education policy and policy research'. *British Education Journal* 23 (3), 257–74.

— (2003) *Class Strategies and the Education Market: The middle classes and social advantage.* London: RoutledgeFalmer.

— (2007) *Education PLC: Understanding private sector participation in public sector education.* Abingdon: Routledge.

— (2013) *Education, Justice and Democracy: The struggle over ignorance and opportunity.* London: Centre for Labour and Social Studies.

Ball, S. and Junemann, C. (2012) *Networks, New Governance and Education.* Bristol: Policy Press.

Ball, S., Maguire, M., and Braun, A. (2012) *How Schools Do Policy: Policy enactments in secondary schools.* Abingdon: Routledge.

Bangs, J., MacBeath, J., and Galton, M. (2011) *Reinventing Schools, Reforming Teaching. From political visions to classroom reality.* Abingdon: Routledge.

Barber, M. (1996) *The Learning Game: Arguments for an education revolution.* London: Victor Gollancz.

— (2008) *Instruction to Deliver: Fighting to transform Britain's public services.* London: Methuen.

— (2015) *How to Run a Government: So that citizens benefit and taxpayers don't go crazy.* London: Penguin Allen Lane.

Barber, M., with Moffit, A., and Kihn, K. (2011) *Deliverology 101: A field guide for educational leaders.* Thousand Oaks, CA: Sage.

Barker, B. (2010) *The Pendulum Swings: Transforming school reform.* Stoke-on-Trent: Trentham Books.

Bathmaker, A-M. and Harnett, P. (eds) (2010) *Exploring Learning, Identity and Power through Life History and Narrative Research.* Abingdon: Routledge.

Belfield, C., Cribb, J., Hood, A., and Joyce, R. (2014) *Living Standards, Poverty and Inequality in the UK: 2014.* London: the Institute for Fiscal Studies. Online. www.ifs.org.uk/uploads/publications/comms/r96.pdf (accessed 26 August 2014).

Bishop, M. and Green, M. (2008) *Philanthrocapitalism: How giving can save the world.* London: Bloomsbury.

Blanden, J., Gregg, P., and Machin, S. (2005) *Intergenerational Mobility in Europe and North America: A report supported by the Sutton Trust.* London: LSE.

Blunkett, D. (2000) *Transforming Secondary Education.* London: The Social Market Foundation.

— (2014) *Review of Education Structures, Functions and the Raising of Standards for All: Putting students and parents first.* London: The Labour Party.

Bottero, W. (2005) *Stratification: Social division and inequality.* Abingdon: Routledge.

Bourdieu, P. and Passeron, J-C. (1977) *Reproduction in Education, Society and Culture.* 2nd ed. London: Sage.

Bourdieu, P. and Wacquant, L. (1992) *An Invitation to Reflexive Sociology.* Cambridge: Polity Press.

Boyask, R. (2015) 'Nuanced Understandings of Privatisation in Local Autorities' Services to Schools'. *Management in Education, 29* (1) 35-40.

Bradley, H. (2014) 'Class descriptors or class relations? Thoughts towards a critique of Savage et al.'. *Sociology*, 48 (3), 429–36.

Brewer, M., Muriel, A., Phillips, D., and Sibieta, L. (2009) *Poverty and Inequality in the UK: 2009.* Institute for Fiscal Studies Commentary C109. London: IFS.

Brown, P. and Lauder, H. (1997) 'Education, globalisation and economic development'. In Halsey *et al.*, 172–92.

Burgess, S. (2014) *Understanding the Success of London's Schools.* Bristol: Centre for Market and Public Organisation, University of Bristol. Online. www.bristol.ac.uk/media-library/sites/cmpo/migrated/documents/wp333.pdf (accessed 5 May 2015).

Burke, E. (2005) *Thoughts on Present Discontents.* Originally 1770. Whitefish, MN: Kessinger Publishing.

Cabinet Office (2010) *The Coalition: Our programme for government.* London: Cabinet Office. Online. http://tinyurl.com/nrjht9d (accessed 19 January 2011).

— (2011) *Opening Doors, Breaking Barriers: A strategy for social mobility.* London: Cabinet Office. Online. http://tinyurl.com/nfujehj (accessed 30 April 2011).

References

Cameron, David (2010) 'We will make government accountable to the people'. Speech made to senior civil servants, July 8. Online. http://tinyurl.com/o9c2x2o (accessed 22 October 2015).

— (2015) 'Opportunity'. Speech delivered 22 June. Online. www.gov.uk/government/speeches/pm-speech-on-opportunity (accessed 30 October 2015).

Carter, A. (2015) *Carter Review of Initial Teacher Training (ITT)*. London: DfE. Online. http://tinyurl.com/o4xhqk3 (accessed 20 March 2015).

Church of England (2013) *A Diocesan Board of Education of the Future*. London: Archbishop's Council Education Division. Online. www.churchofengland.org/media/1794108/cofe%20dbe%20future%20-%20final%20version.pdf (accessed 12 February 2015).

Cingano, F. (2014) 'Trends in income inequality and its impact on economic growth'. *OECD Social, Employment and Migration Working Papers No 163*. Paris: OECD Publishing.

Clarke, P. (ed.) (2005) *Improving Schools in Difficulty*. London: Continuum.

Clifton, J. and Cook, W. (2012) *A Long Division: Closing the attainment gap in England's secondary schools*. London: IPPR. Online. www.ippr.org/files/images/media/files/publication/2012/09/long%20division%20FINAL%20version_9585.pdf?noredirect=1 (accessed 16 November 2013).

Coffield, F. and Williamson, B. (2011) *From Exam Factories to Communities of Discovery*. London: Institute of Education.

Cohen, L., Manion, L., and Morrison, K. (2010) *Research Methods in Education*. 6th ed. Abingdon: Routledge.

Coldron, J., Crawford, M., Jones, S., and Simkins, T. (2014) 'The restructuring of schooling in England: The responses of well-positioned headteachers'. *Educational Management, Administration and Leadership*, 42 (3), 387–403.

Coleman, J., Campbell, E., Hobson, C., McPartland, J., Mood, A., Weinfield, R., and York, R. (1966) *Equality of Educational Opportunity*. Washington, DC: US Government Printing Office.

Connelly, R., Sullivan, A., and Jerrim, J. (2014) *Primary and Secondary Education and Poverty Review*. London: Institute of Education. Online. http://tinyurl.com/nh3yoe8 (accessed 25 May 2015).

Conservative Party (2015) *Strong Leadership, A Clear Economic Plan, A Brighter, More Secure Future: The Conservative Party manifesto, 2015*. London: The Conservative Party. Online. http://tinyurl.com/o5ol44n (accessed 16 May, 2015).

Cook, G. and Muir, R. (eds) (2012) *The Relational State: How recognising the importance of human relationships could revolutionise the role of the state*. London: IPPR. Online. http://tinyurl.com/q9ap6ch (accessed 28 August 2013).

Crossley, D. (2013a) *What Works in Enabling School Improvement? The role of the middle tier: Report on the research findings from the York Local Authority case study*. Slough: NFER. Online. http://tinyurl.com/q7oqw6g (accessed 1 December 2013).

— (2013b) *What Works in Enabling School Improvement? The role of the middle tier: Report on the research findings from the Wigan Local Authority case study*. Slough: NFER. Online. http://tinyurl.com/o3jzuml (accessed 1 December 2013).

Crossley-Holland, J. (2012) *The Future Role of the Local Authority in Education*. London: ADCS.

— (2013a) *What Works in Enabling School Improvement? The role of the middle tier: Report on the research findings from the Brighton and Hove Local* Authority case study. Slough: NFER. Online. http://tinyurl.com/ojryykd (accessed 1 December 2013).

— (2013b*) What Works in Enabling School Improvement? The role of the middle tier: Report on the research findings from the Hertfordshire Local Authority case study.* Slough: NFER. Online. www.nfer.ac.uk/publications/MTSL02/ MSTL02Hertfordshirecasestudy.pdf (accessed 1 December 2013).

— (2013c) *What Works in Enabling School Improvement? The role of the middle tier: Report on the research findings from the Southend Educational Trust case study.* Slough: NFER. Online. www.nfer.ac.uk/publications/MTSL02/ MSTL02Hertfordshirecasestudy.pdf (accessed 1 December 2013).

Crouch, C. (2011) *The Strange Non-Death of Neoliberalism.* Cambridge: Polity Press.

Cruddas, L. (2014) 'Ideas take flight'. *Leader*, 81, 15–17.

Cummings, C., Dyson, A., and Todd, L. (2011) *Beyond the School Gates: Can full service and extended schools overcome disadvantage?* Abingdon: Routledge.

Cunningham, B. (ed.) (2008) *Exploring Professionalism.* London: Institute of Education.

Dardar, A., Baltodano, M., and Torres, R. (2009) *The Critical Pedagogy Reader.* 2nd ed. New York: Routledge.

DCSF (2007) *The Children's Plan: Building brighter futures.* London: The Stationery Office Ltd.

— (2008) *National Challenge: A toolkit for schools and local authorities.* London: DCSF. Online. http://tinyurl.com/nl7q95e (accessed 28 October 2015).

— (2009a) *Your Child, Your Schools, Our Future: Building a 21st century schools system.* London: The Stationery Office Ltd. Online. http://webarchive. nationalarchives.gov.uk/20130401151715/http://www.education.gov.uk/ publications/eOrderingDownload/21st_Century_Schools.pdf (accessed 22 October 2015).

— (2009b) *Deprivation and Education: The evidence on pupils in England, Foundation Stage to Key Stage 4.* London: DCSF.

Denzin, N. and Lincoln, Y. (eds) (2000) *Handbook of Qualitative Research.* 2nd ed. London: Sage.

DfE (2010a) *The Importance of Teaching: Schools White Paper 2010.* London: DfE. Online. http://tinyurl.com/qcast5r (accessed 22 October 2015).

— (2010b) *The Case for Change: November 2010.* London: DfE. Online. www. gov.uk/government/uploads/system/uploads/attachment_data/file/180852/DFE-00564-2010.pdf (accessed 30 August 2011).

— (2014a) *Statistical First Release: GCSE and equivalent attainment by pupil characteristics in England, 2012/13* London: DfE. Online. www.gov.uk/ government/uploads/system/uploads/attachment_data/file/280689/SFR05_2014_ Text_FINAL.pdf (accessed 26 August 2014).

— (2014b) *Consultation on Savings to the Education Services Grant for 2015 to 2016.* London: DfE.

— (2014c) *Annex A: Clarification of Local Authority Statutory Duties Relevant to the Education Services Grant.* London: DfE

References

— (2014d) *National Curriculum Assessments at Key Stage 2 in England, 2014 (Revised)*. London: DfE. Online. http://tinyurl.com/qz3onrg (accessed 19 February 2015).

— (2014e) *Statistical First Release: Schools, pupils and their characteristics, January 2014*. London: DfE. Online. http://tinyurl.com/ozo3mkq (accessed 14 May 2015).

DfEE (1997) *Excellence in Schools: A white paper*. London: The Stationery Office Ltd.

— (1998) *Teachers: Meeting the challenge of change*. London: The Stationery Office Ltd.

— (1999) *Excellence in Cities*. London: DfEE.

— (2001) *Schools: Achieving success*. London: The Stationery Office Ltd.

DfES (2002) *A New Specialist System: Transforming secondary education*. London: DfES.

— (2003) *Transforming London Secondary Schools*. London: DfES.

— (2004a) *Every Child Matters: Change for Children*. Nottingham: DfES.

— (2004b) *A New Relationship with Schools*. London: DfES and Ofsted.

— (2005a) *Higher Standards for All: Better schools for all*. London: DfES.

— (2005b) *Education Improvement Partnerships: Local collaboration for school improvement and better service delivery*. London: DfES.

— (2007) *City Challenge for World Class Education*. London: DfES.

Dorling, D. (2010) *Injustice: Why social inequality persists*. Bristol: Policy Press.

— (2014) *Inequality and the 1%*. London: Verso.

DWP (2015) *Policy Paper – 2010 to 2015 Government Policy: Welfare reform*. London: DWP. Online. http://tinyurl.com/p638zol (accessed 1 July 2015).

Earl, L., Watson, N., Levin, B., Leithwood, K., Fullan, M., and Torrance, N., with Jantzi, D., Mascall, B., and Volante, L. (2003) *Watching Learning 3: Final report of the external evaluation of England's national literacy and numeracy strategies* Toronto: Ontario Institute for Studies in Education, University of Toronto.

Earley, P., Higham, R., Allen, R., Allen, T., Howson, J., Nelson, R., Rawal, S., Lynch, S., Morton, L., Mehta, P., and Sims, D. (2012) *Review of School Leadership*. Nottingham: National College for School Leadership.

Ecclestone, K., Biesta, G., and Hughes, M. (eds) (2010) *Transitions and Learning Through the Lifecourse*. Abingdon: Routledge.

Feinstein, L., Hearn, B., and Renton, Z. with Abrahams, C. and MacLeod, M. (2007) *Reducing Inequalities: Realising the talents of all*. London: National Children's Bureau.

Feinstein, L., Duckworth, K., and Sabates, R. (2008) *Education and the Family: Passing success across the generations*. Abingdon: Routledge.

Fielding, M. and Moss, P. (2011) *Radical Education and the Common School: A democratic alternative*. Abingdon: Routledge.

Fitz, J., Halpin, D., and Power, S. (1993) *Grant Maintained Schools: Education in the market place*. London: Kogan Page.

Fullan, M. (2001) *The New Meaning of Educational Change*. 3rd ed. New York: Teachers College Press.

— (2003) *Change Forces with a Vengeance*. London: RoutledgeFalmer.

Gale, T. (2003) 'Realising policy: The who and how of policy production'. *Discourse: Studies in the cultural politics of education*, 24 (1), 51–65. Also in Lingard and Ozga (2007), 220–35.

Gillborn, D. and Youdell, Y. (2000) *Rationing Education: Policy, practice, reform and equity*. Buckingham: Open University Press.

Glaser, B. and Strauss, A. (1967) *The Discovery of Grounded Theory*. Chicago, IL: Aldane.

Goldthorpe, J. (2007) *Illustration and Retrospect*. Oxford: Oxford University Press. Vol. 2 of *On Sociology*, 2nd ed.

Goodson, I., Biesta, G., Tedder, M., and Adair, N. (2010) *Narrative Learning*. Abingdon: Routledge.

Gorard, S. (2000) *Education and Social Justice: The changing composition of schools and its implications*. Cardiff: University of Wales Press.

Gorard, S., Huat See, B., and Davies, P. (2012) *The Impact of Attitudes and Aspirations on Educational Attainment and Participation*. York: Joseph Rowntree Foundation. Online. http://tinyurl.com/qxnkwx4 (accessed 24 March 2015).

Gray, J., Hopkins, D., Reynolds, D., Wilcox, B., Farrell, S., and Jesson, D. (1999) *Improving Schools: Performance and potential*. Buckingham: Open University Press.

Greany, T. (2014) *Are We Nearly There Yet? Progress, issues, and possible next steps for a self-improving school system: An inaugural professorial lecture*. London: Institute of Education.

— (2015) *The Self-Improving System in England: A review of evidence and thinking*. Leicester: ASCL.

Greany, T. and Brown, C. (2015) *Partnerships between Teaching Schools and Universities: Research support*. London: Institute of Education.

Gregg, P. and Goodman, A. (2010) *Poorer Children's Attainment: How important are attitudes and behaviours?* York: Joseph Rowntree Foundation.

Gunter, H. (2012) *Leadership and the Reform of Education*. Bristol: Policy Press.

Halsey, A., Lauder, H., Brown, P., and Wells, A. (1997) *Education: Culture, economy and society*. Oxford: Oxford University Press.

Hargreaves, D. (2003) *Education Epidemic. Transforming secondary schools through innovation networks*. London: Demos.

— (2010) *Creating a Self-Improving School System*. Nottingham: National College for School Leadership. Online. http://tinyurl.com/q4ltyny (accessed 12 September 2013).

— (2011) *Leading a Self-Improving School System*. Nottingham: National College for School Leadership. Online. http://tinyurl.com/o6t9n95 (accessed 12 September 2013).

— (2012a) *A Self-Improving School System in International Context*. Nottingham: National College for School Leadership. Online. www.gov.uk/government/uploads/system/uploads/attachment_data/file/325905/a-self-improving-system-in-international-context.pdf (accessed 12 September 2013).

— (2012b) *A Self-Improving School System: Towards maturity*. Nottingham: National College for School Leadership. Online. http://tinyurl.com/o865rv4 (accessed 12 September 2013).

References

Harris, A., James, S., Gunraj, J. Clarke, P., and Harris, B. (2006) *Improving Schools in Exceptionally Challenging Circumstances: Tales from the frontline.* London: Continuum.

Harvey, D. (2011) *A Brief History of Neoliberalism.* Originally 2005. Oxford: Oxford University Press.

Hatcher, R. (2014) Local authorities and the school system: The new authority-wide partnerships. *Education, Management and Leadership.* 42 (3), 355–71.

Hill, R. (2011) *The Importance of Teaching and the Role of System Leadership.* Nottingham: National College for School Leadership.

Hills, J., Sefton, T., and Stewart, K. (2009) *Towards a More Equal Society; Poverty, inequality and policy since 1997.* Bristol: Policy Press.

Hills, J., Brewer, M., Jenkins, S., Lister, R., Lupton, R., Machin, S., Mills, C., Modood, T., Rees T., and Riddell, S. (2010) *An Anatomy of Economic Inequality in the UK: Report of the National Equality Panel.* London: Government Equalities Office/Centre for Analysis of Social Exclusion. Online. http://eprints.lse.ac.uk/28344/1/CASEreport60.pdf (accessed 27 August 2014).

Hobsbawm, E. (1995) *The Age of Extremes: The short twentieth century 1914–1991.* London: Abacus.

Holloway, E., Mahony, S., Royston, S., and Mueller, D. (2014) *At What Cost; Exposing the impact of poverty on school life.* London: The Children's Society.

Hopkins, D. (2007) *Every School a Great School: Realising the potential of system leadership.* Maidenhead: McGraw Hill.

Hopkins, D., Reynolds, D., Potter, D., and Chapman, C., with Beresford, J., Jackson, P., Sharpe, T., Singleton, C., and Watts, R. (2001) *Meeting the Challenge: An improvement guide*; *A Handbook of Guidance*; *A Review of Research and Practice* (pack of three booklets). London: DfEE.

Hopkins, D. and Higham, R. (2007) 'System leadership: Mapping the landscape'. *School Leadership and Management.* 27 (2), 147–166.

House of Commons Committee of Public Accounts (2013) *Establishing Free Schools.* London: The Stationery Office Ltd.

— (2015) *School Oversight and Intervention.* London: The Stationery Office Ltd.

House of Commons Education Committee (2015) *Academies and Free Schools: Fourth report of session 2014–15.* London: The Stationery Office Ltd.

Hughes, M., Greenhough, P., Ching Yee, W., and Andrews, J. (2010) 'The daily transition between home and school'. In Ecclestone *et al.* (eds), 16–31.

Husbands, C. (2015) 'What are teaching schools for?' *Management in Education,* 29 (1), 31–4.

Hutchings, M., Greenwood, C., Hollingworth, S., Mansaray, A., Rose, A., Minty, S., and Glass, K. (2012) *Evaluation of the City Challenge Programme.* London: DfE. Online. http://tinyurl.com/o7hmeun (accessed 26 February 2015).

Hutchings, M., Francis, B., and De Vries, R. (2014) *Chain Effects: The impact of academy chains on low income students.* London: The Sutton Trust. Online. www.suttontrust.com/wp-content/uploads/2014/08/chain-effects-july-14-final-1.pdf (accessed 29 June 2015).

Jerrim, J. and Vignoles, A. (2011) *The Use and Misuse of Statistics in Understanding Social Mobility: Regression to the mean and the cognitive development of high ability children from disadvantaged homes.* DoQSS Working Paper No 11–01. London: Institute of Education.

Jones, O. (2014) *The Establishment and How They Get Away With It*. London: Allen Lane.

Kendall, L., O'Donnell, L., Golden, S., Ridley, K., Machin, S., Rutt, S., McNally, S., Schagen, I., Meghir, C., Stoney, S., Morris, M., Weat, A., and Noden, S. (2005) *Excellence in Cities: The national evaluation of a policy to raise standards in urban schools 2000–2003*. London: DfES.

Kerr, K. and West, M. (eds) (2010) *Social Inequality: Can schools narrow the gap?* Macclesfield: BERA. Online. www.bera.ac.uk/wp-content/uploads/2014/01/Insight2-web.pdf?noredirect=1 (accessed 10 January 2014).

Kerr, K., Dyson, A., and Raffo, C. (2014) *Education, Disadvantage and Place: Making the local matter*. Bristol: Policy Press.

Kintrea, K., St Clair, R., and Houston, M. (2011) *The Influence of Place, Parents and Poverty on Educational Attitudes and Aspirations*. York: The Joseph Rowntree Foundation. Online. www.jrf.org.uk/report/influence-parents-places-and-poverty-educational-attitudes-and-aspirations (accessed 26 October 2011).

Lareau, A. (2000) *Home Advantage: Social class and parental intervention in elementary education*. Lanham, MD: Rowman and Littlefield.

Lawn, M. (2013) 'A systemless system: Designing the disarticulation of English state education'. *European Educational Research Journal*, 12 (3), 231–41. Online. http://dx.doi.org/10.2304/eerj.2013.12.2.231

Lawton, K., Cooke, G., and Pearce, N. (2014) *The Condition of Britain: Strategies for social renewal*. London: IPPR.

LeGrand, J. (1997) 'Knights, knaves or pawns; Human behaviour and social policy'. *Journal of Social Policy*, 26 (2), 149–69.

— (2003) *Motivation, Agency and Public Policy: Of knights and knaves, pawns and queens*. Oxford: Oxford University Press.

LGA (2013) *Rewiring Public Services: Rejuvenating democracy*. London: Local Government Association. Online. http://tinyurl.com/pxsral7 (accessed 10 September 2013).

— (2014a) *Investing in Our Nation's Future: The first 100 days of the next government*. London: the Local Government Association. Online. http://tinyurl.com/mude5ak (accessed 28 July 2014).

— (2014b) *Under Pressure: How councils are planning for future cuts*. London: the Local Government Association. Online. http://tinyurl.com/n2yuzxo (accessed 17 June 2015).

LGA/SOLACE (2013) *The Council's Role in School Improvement: Case studies of emerging models*. London: Local Government Association. Online. www.local.gov.uk/c/document_library/get_file?uuid=16b1eed6-afe6-4b60-a65f-c65073f258d4&groupId=10180 (accessed 23 June 2015).

Lingard, B., Ladwig, J., and Luke, A. (1998) 'School effects in postmodern conditions'. In Slee *et al.* (eds), 84–100.

Lingard, B. and Ozga, J. (eds) (2007) *The RoutledgeFalmer Reader in Education Policy and Politics*. London: Routledge.

Lodge, M. and Hood, C. (2012) 'Into an age of multiple austerities? Public management and public service bargains across OECD Countries'. *Governance: An International Journal of Policy, Administration, and Institutions*, 25 (1), 79–101.

References

McCulloch, G. (2001) *Failing the Ordinary Child: The theory and practice of working class secondary education.* Buckingham: Open University Press.

McKinsey (2007) *How the World's Best-Performing School Systems Come Out on Top.* London: McKinsey & Company. Online. http://mckinseyonsociety.com/downloads/reports/Education/Worlds_School_Systems_Final.pdf (accessed 23 November 2010).

— (2010) *How the World's Most Improved School Systems Keep Getting Better.* London: McKinsey & Company. Online. http://mckinseyonsociety.com/downloads/reports/Education/Education_Intro_Standalone_Nov%2026.pdf (accessed 20 July 2011).

Mansell, W. (2014a) 'Regional schools commissioners: Leaked report on academy "advocates"'. *The Guardian*, 22 April.

— (2014b) 'Slowdown in number of schools converting to academies'. *The Guardian,* 28 October.

Marx, K. (1979) 'The Eighteenth Brumaire of Louis Bonaparte'. Originally 1852. *Collected Works* Volume 11. London: Lawrence and Wishart.

Mason, P. (2015) *Postcapitalism: A guide to our future.* London: Allen Lane.

Mayor of London (2012) *The Mayor's Education Inquiry Final Report: Findings and recommendations.* London: Greater London Authority. Online. www.london.gov.uk/sites/default/files/The%20Mayor's%20Education%20Inquiry%20Final%20Report.pdf (accessed 13 May 2015).

Milburn, A. (2009) *Unleashing Aspiration: The final report of the panel on fair access to the professions.* London: The Cabinet Office. Online. http://webarchive.nationalarchives.gov.uk/+/http:/www.cabinetoffice.gov.uk/media/227102/fair-access.pdf (accessed 22 January 2011).

— (2012) *Fair Access to Professional Careers: A Progress Report by the Independent Reviewer on Social Mobility and Child Poverty.* London: The Cabinet Office. Online. https://www.gov.uk/government/uploads/system/uploads/attachment_data/file/61090/IR_FairAccess_acc2.pdf (accessed 5 January 2015).

Miliband, D. (2004) 'Personalised learning: Building a new relationship with schools'. Speech delivered at the North of England Education Conference, Belfast, January. London: DfES. Online. http://tinyurl.com/lz44fog (accessed 12 May 2015).

Mirowski, P. (2013) *Never Let a Serious Crisis Go to Waste: How neoliberalism survived the financial meltdown.* London: Verso.

Morrison, N. (2015) 'Number of teachers quitting the classroom reaches 10-year high'. *Times Educational Supplement*, 30 January.

Muijs, D., Chapman, C., and Armstrong, P. (2012) 'Teach First: Pedagogy and outcomes: The impact of an alternative certification programme'. *Journal for Educational Research Online,* 4 (2), 29–64.

NAO (2013) *Establishing Free Schools.* London: The Stationery Office Ltd. Online. www.nao.org.uk/wp-content/uploads/2013/12/10314-001-Free-Schools-Book.pdf (accessed 14 May 2014).

— (2014) *Performance and Capability of the Education Funding Agency.* London: The Stationery Office Ltd. Online. www.nao.org.uk/wp-content/uploads/2015/01/Performance-and-capability-of-the-Education-Funding-Agency.pdf (accessed 14 May 2014).

— (2015) *Funding for Disadvantaged Pupils.* London: The Stationery Office Ltd. Online. www.nao.org.uk/wp-content/uploads/2015/06/Funding-for-disadvantaged-pupils.pdf (accessed 30 June 2015).

National Research Council (2000) *How People Learn: Brain, mind, experience and school.* Washington DC: National Academy Press.

NCB (2013) *Greater Expectations: Rising aspirations for our children.* London: National Children's Bureau.

NCSL (2002) *Networked Learning Communities: Principles.* Cranfield: National College for School Leadership.

— (2003) *Networked Learning Communities: Briefing paper.* Cranfield: National College for School Leadership.

NFER (2015) *Academies and Maintained Schools: What do we know?* Slough: NFER.

O'Connor, M., Hales, E., Davies, J., and Tomlinson, S. 1998. *Hackney Downs: The school that dared to fight.* London: Falmer Press.

OECD (2007) *The Programme for International Student Assessment (PISA): OECD's latest PISA study of learning skills among 15-year-olds.* Paris: OECD.

— (2010) *PISA 2009 Results – Overcoming Social Background: Equity in learning opportunities and outcomes.* Paris: OECD. Vol. 2 of *PISA 2009 Results.* 6 vols. Paris: OECD. Online. http://dx.doi.org/10.1787/9789264091504-en (accessed 26 August 2014).

— (2011a) *An Overview of Growing Income Inequalities in OECD Countries: Main findings.* Paris: OECD. Online. www.oecd.org/els/soc/49499779.pdf (accessed 4 November 2014).

— (2011b) *Divided We Stand: Why inequality keeps rising* (Country Note: United Kingdom). Paris: OECD. Online. www.oecd.org/els/soc/49170768.pdf (accessed 4 November 2014).

— (2012) 'How long do students spend in the classroom? In *Education at a Glance 2012: Highlights.* Paris: OECD. Online. http://dx.doi.org/10.1787/eag_highlights-2013-en (accessed 15 December 2014).

Ofsted (1997) *From Failure to Success.* London: Ofsted.

— (1999) *Lessons Learned from Special Measures.* London: Ofsted.

— (2001) *Forward from Special Measures.* London: Ofsted.

— (2012) *The Annual Report of Her Majesty's Chief Inspector of Education, Children's Services and Skills 2011–12.* London: The Stationery Office Ltd.

— (2013) *Unseen Children – Access and Achievement 20 Years On: Evidence report.* Manchester: Ofsted. Online. http://tinyurl.com/nsxy2ns (accessed 20 April 2014).

— (2014a) *School Inspection Handbook.* Manchester: Ofsted. Online. http://dera.ioe.ac.uk/19878/1/School%20inspection%20handbook.pdf (accessed 16 August 2014).

— (2014b) *The Report of Her Majesty's Chief Inspector of Education, Children's Services and Skills 2013–14.* Manchester: Ofsted. Online. www.gov.uk/government/uploads/system/uploads/attachment_data/file/384707/Ofsted_Annual_Report_201314_Schools.pdf (accessed 2 July 2015).

References

— (2015a) *Office for Standards in Education, Children's Services and Skills: Annual report and accounts 2014–15*. London: Ofsted. Online. www.gov.uk/government/uploads/system/uploads/attachment_data/file/432859/Ofsted_annual_reports_accounts_2014-15.pdf (accessed 10 June 2015).

— (2015b) *The Future of Education Inspection: Understanding the changes.* Manchester: Ofsted. Online. http://tinyurl.com/na8jfwu (accessed 12 June 2015).

— (2015c) *Ofsted inspections: Clarification for schools.* Manchester: Ofsted.

ONS (2014) *Working and Workless Households*. London: Office for National Statistics. Online. www.ons.gov.uk/ons/dcp171778_382704.pdf (accessed 30 October 2014).

— (2015) *GDP and the Labour Market: Q1 2015 quarterly update*. London: ONS. Online. www.ons.gov.uk/ons/dcp171780_403544.pdf (accessed 1 July 2014).

Ozga, J. (2009) 'Governing education through data in England: From regulation to self-evaluation'. *Journal of Education Policy*, 24 (2), 149–62.

— (2012) 'Governing knowledge: Data, inspection and education policy in Europe'. *Globalisation, Societies and Education*, 10 (4), 439–55.

Parish, N., Baxter, A., and Sandals, L. (2012) *Action Research into the Evolving Role of the Local Authority*. London: DfE. Online. www.gov.uk/government/uploads/system/uploads/attachment_data/file/184055/DFE-RR224.pdf (accessed 26 May 2015).

Pollock, A. and Price, D. (2013) *Duty to Care: In defence of universal health care.* London: Centre for Labour and Social Studies. Online. http://classonline.org.uk/docs/2013_05_Policy_Paper_-_A_duty_to_care_(Allyson_Pollock__David_Price).pdf (accessed 4 May 2015).

Porter, N. and Simons, J. (2015) *A Rising Tide: The competitive benefits of free schools.* London: Policy Exchange. Online. www.policyexchange.org.uk/images/publications/a%20rising%20tide.pdf (accessed 30 March 2015).

Power, S., Rees, G., and Taylor, C. (2005) 'New Labour and educational disadvantage: The limits of area-based initiatives'. *London Review of Education*, 3 (2), 101–16.

Power, S. and Whitty, G. (2008) *Graduating and Graduations within the Middle Class: The legacy of an elite higher education.* Cardiff: Cardiff University School of Social Sciences. Online. www.cardiff.ac.uk/socsi/resources/wp118.pdf (accessed 1 July 2015).

Pritchard, D. (2012) *Schools Causing Concern: A research project.* London: ADCS. Online. http://tinyurl.com/nestext (accessed 14 August 2012).

Rasbash, J., Leckie, G., Pillinger, R., and Jenkins, J. (2010) 'Children's educational progress: Positioning family, school and area effects'. *Journal of the Royal Statistical Society*, 173 (3) 657–82.

Raymond, E. (2001) *The Cathedral and the Bazaar: Musings on Linux and open source by an accidental revolutionary.* Sebastapol, CA: O'Reilly Media.

Rea, S., Hill, R., and Dunford, J. (2013) *Closing the Gap: How system leaders can work together.* London: National College for Teaching and Leadership.

Reynolds, D. and Farrell, S. (1996) *Worlds Apart; A review of international surveys of educational achievement involving England.* London: Ofsted.

Riddell, R. (2003) *Schools for Our Cities: Urban learning for the twenty-first century.* Stoke-on-Trent: Trentham Books.

— (2009) 'Schools in trouble again: A critique of the National Challenge (2008)'. *Improving Schools,* 12 (1), 71–80.

— (2010) *Aspiration, Identity and Self-Belief: Snapshots of social structure at work.* Stoke-on-Trent: Trentham Books.

— (2013) 'Changing policy levers under the neoliberal state: Realising coalition policy on education and social mobility'. *Journal of Education Policy,* 28 (6), 847–63.

Ridge, T. (2006) 'Childhood poverty: A barrier to social participation and inclusion'. In Tisdall *et al.* (eds), 23–38.

Rudd, P., Poet, H., Featherstone, G., Lamont, E., Durbin, B., Bergeron, C., Kettlewell, K., and Hart, R. (2011) *Evaluation of City Challenge Leadership Strategies: Overview report.* Slough: NFER.

Rutter, M., Maughan, B., Mortimore, P., and Ouston, J. (1979) *Fifteen Thousand Hours: Secondary schools and their effects on children.* Shepton Mallet: Open Books.

Sammons, P., Hillman, J., and Mortimore, P. (1995) *Key Characteristics of Effective Schools: A review of school effectiveness research.* London: Institute of Education; Ofsted.

Sampson, A. (2004) *Who Runs this Place? The Anatomy of Britain in the twenty-first century.* London: John Murray.

Savage, M., Devine, F., Cunningham, N., Taylor, M., Li, Y., Hjellbrekke, J., Le Roux, B., Friedman, S., and Miles, A. (2013) 'A new model of social class? Findings from the BBC's Great British Class Survey'. *Sociology,* 47 (2), 219–50.

Simkins, T. (2015) 'School restructuring in England: New school configurations and new challenges'. *Management in Education,* 29 (1), 4–8.

Simkins, T., Coldron, J., Crawford, M., and Jones, S. (2014) 'Emerging local schooling landscapes: The role of the local authority'. *School Leadership and Management,* 35 (1), 1–16. Online. http://dx.doi.org/10.1080/13632434.2 014.962501

Siraj-Blatchford. I. (2010) 'Learning in the home and at school: How working class children "succeed against the odds"'. *British Educational Research Journal,* 36 (3), 463–82.

Skeggs, B. (2004) *Class, Self, Culture.* London: Routledge.

Slee, R. and Weiner, G., with Tomlinson, S. (eds) (1998) *School Effectiveness for Whom; Challenges to the school effectiveness and school improvement movements.* London: Falmer Press.

Smith, R., Aston, H., Sims, D., and Easton, C. (2012) *Enabling School-driven System Leadership.* Slough: NFER. Online. www.nfer.ac.uk/publications/ MTSL01/MTSL01.pdf (accessed 13 August 2014).

Social Exclusion Unit (2001) *A New Commitment to Neighbourhood Renewal – National Strategy Action Plan.* London: The Social Exclusion Unit.

Social Mobility and Child Poverty Commission (2014) *State of the Nation 2014: Social mobility and child poverty in the UK.* London: SMCP Commission.

Stewart, W. (2014) 'Is Ofsted's grading scandalous; Inspectors judge schools on pupils' ability, analysis shows'. *Times Educational Supplement,* 22 August.

References

Stoll, L. (2015) *Three Greats for a Self-improving School System – Pedagogy, Professional Development and Leadership: Teaching schools R&D network national themes project 2012–14*. London: National College for Teaching and Leadership.

Stoll, L. and Fink, D. (1995) *Changing Our Schools*. Buckingham: Open University Press.

Stoll, L. and Myers, K. (eds) (1998) *No Quick Fixes: Perspectives on schools in difficulty*. London: Falmer Press.

Strand, S. (2010) 'Do some schools narrow the gap? Differential school effectiveness by ethnicity, gender, poverty, and prior achievement'. *School Effectiveness and* School *Improvement*, 21 (3), 289–314.

— (2014a) 'School effects and ethnic, gender and socio-economic gaps in educational achievement at age 11'. *Oxford Review of Education*, 40 (2), 223–45.

— (2014b) 'Ethnicity, gender, social class and achievement gaps at age 16: Intersectionality and "getting it" for the white working class'. *Research Papers in Education*, 29 (2),131–71.

Sylva, K., Melhuish, E., Sammons, P., Siraj-Blatchford, I., and Taggart, B. (2010) *Early Childhood Matters: Evidence from the effective pre-school and primary education project*. Abingdon: Routledge.

Teddlie, C. and Stringfield, S. (1993) *Schools Make a Difference: Lessons learned from a ten-year study of school effects*. New York: Teachers College Press.

Thomas, G. and James, D. (2006) 'Reinventing grounded theory: Some questions about theory, ground and discovery'. *British Educational Research Journal*, 32 (6), 767–95.

Tisdall, E., Davis, J., Hill, M., and Prout, A. (2006) *Children, Young People and Social Inclusion: Participation for what?*. Bristol: Policy Press.

Tomlinson, S. (1998) *A Tale of One School in One City: Hackney Downs*. In Slee *et al.* (eds), 157–69.

Vaughan, R. (2014) 'Nicky Morgan says academies are "just part of the picture", as charm offensive continues'. *Times Educational Supplement*, 15 August. Online. http://tinyurl.com/q2dw5xr (accessed 30 October 2015).

— (2015) 'Ofsted purges more than 1,200 inspectors'. *Times Educational Supplement*, 19 June.

Vincent, C. and Ball, S. (2007) '"Making up" the middle class child: Families, activities and class dispositions'. *Sociology*, 41 (6), 1,061–77.

Vincent, C., Ball, S., Rollock, N., and Gillborn, D. (2013) 'Raising middle class black children: Parenting priorities, actions and strategies'. *Sociology*, 47 (3), 427–42.

Whitty, G. (2002) *Making Sense of Education Policy*. London: Paul Chapman.

— (2008) 'Changing modes of teacher professionalism: Traditional, managerial, collaborative and democratic'. In Cunningham (ed.), 28–49.

Whitty, G. and Anders, J. (2013) *(How) Did New Labour Narrow the Achievement and Participation Gap?* London: Institute of Education; Centre for Learning and Life Chances in Knowledge Economies and Societies.

Whitty, G., Power, S., and Halpin, D. (1998) *Devolution and Choice in Education: The school, the state and the market*. Buckingham: Open University Press.

Wiborg, S. (2010) *Swedish Free Schools: Do they work?* London: Institute of Education; Centre for Learning and Life Chances in Knowledge Economies and Societies.

Wilkinson, R. and Pickett, K. (2009) *The Spirit Level: Why more equal societies almost always do better*. London: Allen Lane.

Woods, D., Husbands, C., and Brown, C. (2013) *Transforming Education for All: The Tower Hamlets story*. London: Tower Hamlets Communications Unit.

Wrigley, T. (2003) *Schools of Hope: A new agenda for school improvement*. Stoke-on-Trent: Trentham Books.

Wrigley, T., Thomson, P., and Lingard, B. (2012) *Changing Schools: Alternative ways to make a difference*. Abingdon: Routledge.

Young, T. (2014) *Prisoners of the Blob: Why most education experts are wrong about nearly everything*. London: Civitas.

Index